INDIVIDUATION

INDIVIDUATION

*A Study of the Depth Psychology of
Carl Gustav Jung*

by

JOSEF GOLDBRUNNER

UNIVERSITY OF NOTRE DAME PRESS • 1964

This translation from the original German, Individuation:
Die Tiefenpsychologie von Carl Gustav Jung (*Erich
Wewel Verlag Krailling vor München*), *was made by*
STANLEY GODMAN

First Paperback Edition
Copyright © 1964 by the

University of Notre Dame Press
Notre Dame, Indiana

Second Printing
January 1965

Reprinted under license agreement with
Erich Wewel Publishing House, Freiburg, Germany

MANUFACTURED IN THE UNITED STATES OF AMERICA BY
NORTH STATE PRESS, INC., HAMMOND, INDIANA

CONTENTS

CONTENTS

PREFACE

THE psychological discovery of the unconscious in the psyche represents a momentous and fruitful extension of our knowledge of man. Doctors drew attention to it; psychotherapists tried to construct a psychology which would penetrate the unconscious depths of the psyche. But it was only under Carl Gustav Jung's leadership that the basis of the new psychology was extended and disengaged from neurology. Psychotherapy led to the development of depth psychology. Medical treatment provided the necessary impulse for a penetration into the depths of the psyche and a comprehensive psychology of culture. Hypnosis, catharsis and analysis, the cure of neuroses, strains and complexes are no longer regarded as the sole task of psychotherapy: the power to help and guide the soul is the claim that is now made. 'The change is significant since it puts the whole knowledge and equipment of psychotherapy which constant practice has developed, refined and systematized, at the service of self-education and self-perfection, and analytical psychology has thereby broken the chains that have tied it to the doctor's consultation room.' A psychological wave is vibrating through the human race. According to an enquiry conducted by C. G. Jung people prefer to consult a psychotherapist rather than a clergyman in their spiritual need. A secularized ministry is now competing with the religious ministry. 'A third of my patients', Jung declares, 'suffer not from any clinically definable neurosis but from the meaninglessness and triviality of their lives.' Therapeutics of the soul have developed into a science of the welfare of the soul. The fruits of this work are a method for the building up of the individual personality and a psychology of personality.

Psychotherapy has thus abandoned its original starting point, purely psychic illness, it has loosened its connections with the abnormal, and disengaged itself from medicine in general and psychiatry in particular. This development means that the psychopathologist and the medical doctor no longer enjoy a monopoly in matters of depth psychology. Psychology, philosophy and theology have been drawn into the study of these questions. The life of the healthy soul and no longer merely the diseased soul is now being investigated, extended and sifted with the resources discovered by psychotherapy. New aspects of religious experience and education have also been opened up. The insights of depth psychology are being incorporated into anthropology.

This is the attitude from which we propose to examine the work of C. G. Jung. The work is divided into two parts: the exposition of his doctrine—and a critical discussion. The significance of depth psychology for education and the cure of souls will be briefly sketched at the end of the work. A detailed enquiry into this aspect of the subject will appear in a further work.

NOTE TO THE AMERICAN EDITION

Because the translator has for the most part retained the citations to Jung's works in German, the following key is supplied, giving English equivalents to the footnote references. "C.W." indicates the volumes in the Collected Works of Jung, published by Pantheon Books for the Bollingen Foundation in the translation of R. F. C. Hull. References to volumes not yet published, for which no other English version exists, are given in brackets. These other editions of Jung in English are also cited:

Contributions to Analytical Psychology, tr. H. G. and C. F. Baynes, New York and London, 1928.

The Integration of Personality, tr. Stanley Dell, New York and London, 1940.

Modern Man in Search of a Soul, tr. C. F. Baynes, cited in Harvest Books paperbound edn., New York, 1955.

Psychological Types, tr. H. G. Baynes, New York and London, 1923.

Psychology and Religion, New Haven and Oxford, 1938.

The Secret of the Golden Flower, tr. C. F. Baynes, New York and London, 1931.

(The Hull translation of *Two Essays on Analytical Psychology* is also available in a paperbound edn., Meridian Books, 1956, with different pagination.)

Page
5   [1] *Two Essays* (C.W. 7), p. 34.
6   [1] Ibid., p. 39.
10 [2] *Psychological Types* (1923 edn.), ch. V.
12 [1] ["Psychological Typology," in ibid. (C.W. 6).]
14 [1] "Spirit and Life," in *Contributions*, p. 82.
15 [1] *Psychology and Religion* (1938 edn.), pp. 91f.
17 [1] *The Development of Personality* (C.W. 17), p. 108.
18 [1] Ibid., pp. 65ff.
21 [1] *Two Essays* (C.W. 7), p. 265.
23 [1] ["The Theory of Psychoanalysis," in *Freud and Psychoanalysis* (C.W. 4).]
24 [1] *Two Essays* (C.W. 7), pp. 29ff.
26 [1] *The Development of Personality* (C.W. 17), p. 81.
28 [1] "Psychotherapists or the Clergy," in *Modern Man* (H.B.), pp. 229ff.
29 [1] Ibid., p. 234.
30 [1] Ibid., p. 238.
31 [1] Ibid., pp. 239f.
    [2] Ibid., p. 241.

Page
37   ¹ ["General Aspects of Dream Psychology," in *The Structure and Dynamics
        of the Psyche* (C.W. 8).]
38   ¹ [Ibid.]
39   ¹, ² [Ibid.]
43   ¹ *Two Essays* (C.W. 7), p. 41.
44   ¹ Ibid., p. 40.
47   ¹ ["Psychological Typology," in *Psychological Types* (C.W. 6).]
48   ¹ [Ibid.]
49   ¹ *Two Essays* (C.W. 7), pp. 57f.
50   ¹ Ibid., p. 58.
51   ¹ "On Psychical Energy," in *Contributions*, pp. 34ff.
53   ¹ Ibid., pp. 31f.
56   ¹ *Psychological Types* (1923 edn.), p. 616.
58   ¹ *Two Essays* (C.W. 7), p. 51.
     ² Ibid., p. 126.
60   *The Transmutation of Symbols* is an error for *Symbols of Transformation* (C.W.
        5).
63   ¹ *Two Essays* (C.W. 7), p. 89.
     ² Ibid., p. 128.
66   ² Ibid., pp. 134f.
67   ¹ Ibid., p. 135.
     ² Ibid., p. 158.
68   ¹, ² The Introduction to the 1936 *Jahrbuch* was by Olga Froebe-Kapteyn.
        The Eranos Yearbooks, originally published in Zurich, are now being
        partially published in English in Bollingen Series. Cf. 1, *Spirit and
        Nature*; 2, *The Mysteries*; 3, *Man and Time*.
69   ¹ *Psychology of the Unconscious*, p. 149. (The passage is omitted in the re-
        vision, *Symbols of Transformation*.)
70   ¹ In *Contributions*, p. 47.
     ² *Symbols of Transformation* (C.W. 5), p. 335 (rather altered).
71   ¹ "Mind and the Earth," in *Contributions*, p. 112.
72   ¹ *Psychology and Alchemy* (C.W. 12), p. 325.
74   ¹ "Mind and the Earth," in *Contributions*, p. 114.
76   ¹ *Psychology and Alchemy* (C.W. 12), p. 234.
     ² Ibid., pp. 243f.
     ³ Ibid., p. 246.
78   ¹ "Mind and the Earth," in *Contributions*, pp. 108f.
79   ² Ibid., pp. 102f.
82   ¹ *Psychological Types* (1923 edn.), p. 624.
     ² In *Nimbus* (London), autumn, 1953. [And in *The Spirit in Man, Art, and
        Literature*, C.W. 15.]
     ³ ["The Meaning of Psychology for Modern Man," in *Civilization in Transi-
        tion* (C.W. 10).]
83   [Jung's commentaries on *The Tibetan Book of the Dead* and *The Tibetan Book
        of the Great Liberation* and his foreword to Suzuki's *Introduction to Zen
        Buddhism* will be in *Psychology and Religion* (C.W. 11).]
85   ¹ Cf. note for p. 83, above.
88   ¹ By Olga Froebe-Kapteyn.
90   ¹ *Two Essays* (C.W. 7), p. 90.
92   ¹ Ibid., p. 144.
94   ¹ Ibid., p. 171.

Page
96 [1] *Ibid.*, pp. 211ff.
97 [1] The illustrations are collected with additions in Jung's *Gestaltungen des Unbewussten* (Zurich, 1950). [To appear in *Archetypes and the Collective Unconscious* (C.W. 9, i).]
98 [1] *Two Essays* (C.W. 7), p. 215.
100 [1] *Ibid.*, p. 217.
101 [1] *Ibid.*, p. 212.
102 [1] ["General Aspects of Dream Psychology," in *The Structure and Dynamics of the Psyche* (C.W. 8).]
105 [1] *Two Essays* (C.W. 7), pp. 188f.
    [2] ["Concerning the Archetypes," in *Archetypes and the Collective Unconscious* (C.W. 9, i).]
107 [1] "Instinct and Unconscious," in *Contributions*, pp. 270ff.
    [2] "Archetypes of the Collective Unconscious," in *Integration*, pp. 54f.
108 [1] "The Basic Postulates of Analytical Psychology," in *Modern Man* (H.B.), p. 186.
    [2] ["The Soul and Death," in *The Structure and Dynamics of the Psyche* (C.W. 8).]
110 [1] *Modern Man* (H.B.), p. 229.
112 [1] *The Practice of Psychotherapy* (C.W. 16), p. 146.
113 [1] "Archetypes of the Collective Unconscious," in *Integration*, p. 80.
114 [1] "Mind and the Earth," in *Contributions*, pp. 118f.
117 [1] "Archetypes of the Collective Unconscious," *passim*, in *Integration*.
119 [1] *Two Essays* (C.W. 7), p. 219.
120 [1] *Ibid.*, p. 192.
122 [1] *Ibid.*, p. 176.
125 [1] ["Concerning the Archetypes," in *Archetypes and the Collective Unconscious* (C.W. 9, i).]
128 [1] *Two Essays* (C.W. 7), p. 199.
130 [1] *Ibid.*, p. 194.
134 [1] *Ibid.*, p. 117.
135 [1] "The Spiritual Problem of Modern Man," *passim*, in *Modern Man* (H.B.).
139 [1] "On the Relation of Analytical Psychology to Poetic Art," in *Contributions*, p. 247.
140 [1] *Ibid.*, p. 248.
141 [1] See note for p. 97, above.
142 [1] *Two Essays* (C.W. 7), p. 226.
144 [1] *Ibid.*, pp. 219f.
    [2] Commentary to *The Secret of the Golden Flower* (1931 edn.), p. 88.
145 [1] *Two Essays* (C.W. 7), p. 224.
    [2] *Ibid.*, p. 236.
    [3] Commentary to *The Secret of the Golden Flower* (1931 edn.), p. 133.
146 [1] "Spirit and Life," in *Contributions*, p. 87.
    [2] ["General Aspects of Dream Psychology," in *The Structure and Dynamics of the Psyche* (C.W. 8).]
147 [1] ["The Meaning of Psychology for Modern Man," in *Civilization in Transition* (C.W. 10).]
    [2] *The Practice of Psychotherapy* (C.W. 16), p. 46.
    [3] ["General Aspects of Dream Psychology," in *The Structure and Dynamics of the Psyche* (C.W. 8).]

Page
148 [1] ["The Soul and Death," in *The Structure and Dynamics of the Psyche* (C.W. 8).]
     [2] [Ibid.]
     [3] "Stages of Life," in *Modern Man* (H.B.), p. 113.
149 [1] Ibid.
     [2] ["Concerning the Archetypes," in *Archetypes and the Collective Unconscious* (C.W. 9, i).]
     [3] "Psychotherapists or the Clergy," in *Modern Man* (H.B.), p. 244.
151 [2] "Brother Klaus," in *Journal of Nervous and Mental Disease* (New York), April, 1946. [Also in *Psychology and Religion* (C.W. 11).]
152 [1] *Two Essays* (C.W. 7), p. 220.
153 [2] For "Brother Klaus," see note on p. 151, above.
154 [1] Incorrect ref., but cf. "The Lapis-Christus Parallel," in *Psychology and Alchemy* (C.W. 12), pp. 332ff.
     [2] *The Development of Personality* (C.W. 17), p. 180. Other ref. in Swiss edn. of *Psychologie und Religion* only. [Cf. C.W. 11.]
155 [2] Incorrect ref., but cf. "The Spiritual Problem of Modern Man," passim, in *Modern Man* (H.B.).
159 [1] ["Analytical Psychology and Weltanschauung," in *The Structure and Dynamics of the Psyche* (C.W. 8).]
161 [1] *Two Essays* (C.W. 7), p. 70.
162 [1] *The Practice of Psychotherapy* (C.W. 16), p. 17.
163 [1] ["The Soul and Death," in *The Structure and Dynamics of the Psyche* (C.W. 8).]
     [2] *Psychology and Religion* (1938 edn.), p. 57.
165 [1] *Symbols of Transformation* (C.W. 5), pp. 66ff.
     [2] *The Practice of Psychotherapy* (C.W. 16), pp. 36ff.
167 [1] Commentary to *The Secret of the Golden Flower* (1931 edn.), pp. 77ff.
     [2] *Psychology and Religion* (1938 edn.), p. 53.
168 [2] "The Spiritual Problem of Modern Man," in *Modern Man* (H.B.), pp. 203f.
     [3] See n. 2 on p. 82, above.
169 [1] *Two Essays* (C.W. 7), p. 97.
     [2] *Psychology and Religion* (1938 edn.), pp. 78ff.
170 [1] Ibid., pp. 99.
     [2] Ibid., p. 98.
     [3] *Psychological Types*, p. 300.
     [4] [Introduction to the *Tibetan Book of the Dead*, in *Psychology and Religion* (C.W. 11).]
172 [1] ["Concerning the Archetypes," in *Archetypes and the Collective Unconscious* (C.W. 9, i).]
     [2] *Psychology and Religion* (1938 edn.), p. 73.
174 [1] Ibid., pp. 99ff.
183 [1] By Olga Froebe-Kapteyn.

PART ONE

CHAPTER ONE

CARL GUSTAV JUNG'S
POINT OF DEPARTURE

UNTIL the end of the nineteenth century psychology was primarily concerned with the conscious mind. Since the psyche was identified with consciousness, the irrational, hidden and instinctive strata of the mind were neglected and regarded as inferior. Attention was concentrated on the bright, conscious daytime of the human spirit; the night-time of the soul, the dark, turbid unconscious was first exposed by Sigmund Freud at the beginning of the twentieth century. In the age of the Enlightenment and the period that succeeded it the irrational had been buried by over-emphasis on the rational but in the darkness of the unconscious it had produced strange, variegated blossomings. Freud put his finger on the tumours of the neglected unconscious when his patients' sufferings drove him to it. He was forced to rediscover the irrational powers of the soul. He shone a light into man's 'night-life' and found that the life of the soul reaches out beyond consciousness. Consciousness is merely the patch of land illuminated by the conscious mind; all the rest lies in darkness, though it is in fact no less real and active. Freud was forced to draw this inference by the fact that psychic remedies enabled him to cure neuroses. By treating spiritual disease he found that he was able to cure physical troubles too. This meant a radical departure from a psychology exclusively concerned with the activities of the conscious mind. There is a life of the soul that cannot be explained by the contents of consciousness. Freud called it the Unconscious and by so doing he roused the medical materialists of the day into active opposition and the fight against Freud and his 'psychoanalysis' continues unabated to the present day.

Admittedly, Freud himself gave cause for resistance to his theories. He had discovered sex as an active constituent of the soul in the unconscious and identified it with the Unconscious: he was blind to any further continents still awaiting exploration in the dark universe of the soul. He took the part for the whole and made it absolute. 'Once a tooth really aches', as Jung has said, 'the whole soul seems to consist of toothache.' Freud carried his theory to extremes when he declared that sexuality is the only active force in the soul to which everything else can be traced back. His pan-sexualism is like a pendulum swinging to one extreme; it can only be understood at all as a reaction to the opposite extreme of rationalism. He sees the sexual instinct in man as the ever gushing spring, watering the whole land of the spirit.

Freud's most successful opponent was one of his own pupils, the Viennese doctor Alfred Adler. He came from the depths of society, with the career of a street arab behind him. He knew the influence of environment and human society from his own experience. He saw the eternal opposition between the individual's upsurging energies and the downward-dragging, levelling influences of society as the key to man's spiritual life. He considers the diseases of the spirit from the sociological point of view and teaches that man's spiritual life must be conceived as an attempt to stake a claim against the demands which life makes upon him. The tension between the requirements of society and the claims of the individual, between the sense of community and the sense of personality often has results of which the individual is not conscious—this is the assumption which Adler takes over from and shares with Freud. He sees man's spiritual life as an antithesis between the self and the world, between the individual striving for power and the compulsions of society. One or the other force works itself out unconsciously and forms a non-conscious guiding image of which the conscious mind becomes the mere plaything. To become healthy and well-adjusted man must become conscious of the guiding image and come to terms with the reality which confronts the conscious mind. Like Freud, Adler makes a fundamental error. He claims to understand man from one particular angle: he turns one part of man's total make-up, the will to power, into an absolute, just as Freud makes the sexual instinct absolute. Adler bases his theory on human striving: he looks to the end, whereas Freud looks to the beginnings. 'With Freud the life of the soul is a strictly causal succession of facts; with Adler it is an arrangement conditioned by the end.'[1]

Both thinkers are the centre of great schools: psychoanalysis and individual psychology, which have had an important influence on practical medicine. Orthodox medicine is, however, still very largely opposed to any kind of psychotherapy; but the tide has begun to turn and the successes achieved by both schools can no longer be ignored; they have proved the correctness of the working hypothesis that man's spiritual life is made up of a conscious and unconscious part. The unconscious has enabled us to look into the depths of the soul; undreamt-of perspectives have been opened up and psychologists and doctors have glimpsed a foreshadowing of the depth psychology of the future.

The one-sidedness of the two schools made further

[1] *Das Unbewusste im normalen und kranken Seelenleben*, p. 51.

research imperative. Each branded the other as heretical; each made its own creed absolute and final. 'In one case love and its destiny is the supreme and most important fact; in the other, the power of the ego. In the first case the ego is merely a kind of appendage to the love instinct, in the second love is merely a means to the end of getting to the top. Those who are interested in the power of the ego revolt against the first conception; those who are interested in Love will never reconcile themselves to the latter.'[1]

For Freud the diseases of the soul are simply a psychically conditioned disturbance of the sexual instinct; for Adler they are a disturbance of the will to dominate. The antitheses cry out for a synthesis from a higher point of view, which will include and embrace them both and clear the way for new research. Neither school has solved all the mysteries of the soul. Both methods have often failed. Life refuses to be squeezed into narrow categories; it cannot be explained simply in terms of the sex and power instincts. There must be other pairs of opposites besides instinct and reason, self and society. Neither school bored down deep enough into the soul. Where then was the treasure-seeker who would continue the task?

Characteristically, he appeared in one of the quiet countries of Europe which is also a meeting-place for the whole world: Switzerland. People looking for recreation, relaxation and healing in that country were material, ready to hand, for the new depth psychology. 'For thirty years I have known the intimate spiritual life of many hundreds of educated people, sick as well as sound, from the whole civilized world of the white man and it is from this experience that I speak.' These are the words of Carl

[1] *Analytische Psychologie und Erziehung*, p. 63.

Gustav Jung, the psychiatrist, doctor and psychotherapist who is the centre of the Zürich school which stands alongside the other two. This school first appeared under the name of 'analytical psychology' but as it developed further, the term 'complex psychology' became current.

CHAPTER TWO

THE REALITY OF THE PSYCHE

THE key to an understanding of Jung's enquiries is self-experience. The basic experience of man today is the subject-object relationship. Things confront man and wait for his transmuting activity. Out of this mutual relationship the 'work' of man is born. This correlation stamps its image on the psyche. Our consciousness occupies itself with objects; the conscious work of the intellect, the will and the heart is applied to the 'fantasy image' of the objects which confront man and decision presses outwards into actions. The outside rushes in upon us and we confront it. This daily encounter between the external world and our activities forms inside us a conception of reality as that which is effective. We are convinced of the reality of the object, of the active and effective objectivity of the outside world and of our active subjectivity. It is like a bridge of which the piers—the ego and the World—have dug themselves deep down into our consciousness, as a life-begetting tension and polarity.

But this polarity of subject and object suffers a stab in the back within the psyche. A third factor appears, a shattering blow falls from an unknown hand. The desire for action is suddenly inexplicably lost. A headache suddenly prevents us from remembering what we wanted to remember at all costs; we look forward to sleep and sleep is as it were spirited away; we sleep and fantastic images disturb our slumbers; anxiety makes work difficult; insecurity and dizziness cripple all activity; it is as if we were no longer master of our own self. We cannot suppress most of our emotions, we cannot change a bad mood into a good one, we cannot summon or abolish dreams. Even the most intelligent man can sometimes be obsessed by ideas which he cannot master even with the greatest effort of the will. Our memory can make the wildest leaps and bounds: a feat which we can only helplessly admire; fantastic ideas can come into our heads which we have neither sought nor expected. All this can invade consciousness, more or less intensely, though after a period of exacting conscious effort it comes with greater force, compelling our attention. It might appear as if the polarity of subject and object were dissolved into a threefold relationship that can best be expressed in the image of the hammer and anvil, between which the self finds itself passive and defenceless. May we therefore speak of an outer and inner reality, both of which invade the self? Must all the dark happenings of the inner spirit be recognized as an independent reality, although they are related to the self and to the total contents of consciousness? The presentiment of an inner world appears. It is not an unknown world: we are in touch with it every day of our lives. It is usually assigned to the mind, that is, associated with consciousness. But doubts about the validity of this explanation begin to stir once the phenomena become more powerful and independent, confront the ego objectively and oppress consciousness. They are felt to be foreign invaders in the otherwise so familiar inventory of the ego; in fact they are able to take possession of it with frightening power, inundating and dragging along everything else, as though obeying laws of their own. 'When brutal natural forces break through like an earthquake and destroy everything, when inner fires burn like a volcano constantly pressing outwards, then we see that the things of the mind are only a superstructure that can be easily shattered from below.'[1] We can study the autonomy of this invading force in daily life in the passions that force us to submit in spite of the most strenuous efforts to repress them. Language has characteristic ways of expressing this fact of experience: 'I don't know what has come over him today; the devil himself seems to have entered him; it's come over him again; he is beside himself; he's acting like a man possessed.' Primitive man sought the explanation of these strange autonomous passions in external causes, attributing these 'promptings' to evil spirits, demons and the devil himself. An internal process is externalized—projected outside itself. But as soon as we shift the cause to our own inward self, the belief in evil spirits inevitably falls to the ground; we are forced to look for the source in ourselves and to extend the concept of the soul beyond the ego. Where do these dark, spontaneous and autonomous forces spring from, what is the impenetrable water from which they slowly coil their way like bubbles of poison, bursting and poisoning the atmosphere of the soul?

In psychotherapy the following hypothesis has been established: this dark, turbid source is a part of the psyche. It contains the same psychic life as is present in consciousness, but it is subterranean and beyond the searchlight of consciousness, though active and therefore real. 'I must point out that experience shows that the contents of consciousness make the same claim to be real, in relation to the activity of consciousness, by dint of their obstinacy and persistence, as the real things of the external world.'[2]

[1] Werner Schoellgen, *Psychotherapie und sakramentale Beicht*, in *Catholica*, I/1932, p. 150.

[2] *Psychologische Typen*, p. 242.

Recognition of an inner world, of the reality of the psyche, and the extension of the concept of the soul beyond the ego, joining the unconscious to the conscious —this is the key to Jung's psychological thought and the methodical starting-point for a fruitful investigation of the human psyche as a whole.

CHAPTER THREE

THE PERSONAL UNCONSCIOUS

APART from the writings of Freud's imitators, all works on psychotherapy exert a strange influence of their own on the reader which it is difficult to escape from unless sheer prejudice prevents one following and appreciating the line of thought. There are several reasons for this mysterious spell. The seeker after self-understanding does not find here the dry, coldly calculating and strictly 'scientific' facts that appear in the textbooks of academic psychology; instead, he feels something of the activity, emotions, experience and development of real life. The approach is dynamic, not academically static; the soul is not enmeshed in a logically constructed system. The enquiry and the exposition are concerned with the life of the psyche; there is life itself in the books of the depth psychologists. Jung makes a sharp distinction between his own work and the usual kind of psychic research which he calls 'psychology without a soul', which is only concerned with laboratory experiments: its first need is to turn to the reality of the human soul. 'Until recently psychology was just as arbitrary a product of the imagination as medieval science.'[1] Psychotherapy penetrates the depths of the soul: it is concerned with the centre of man; it holds converse with the innermost life of the soul and it alone is psychology in the true sense of the word.

It is true that our lives are deeply involved in the soul but how unfamiliar it is and how foreign the impulses

[1] *Seelenprobleme der Gegenwart*, p. 118.

that rise from the ground of the soul appear! They often seem like an invasion from the unconscious, like a breakthrough into the armoured fortress of the ego, penetrating its walls like X-rays. The ego feels so unprotected and vulnerable.

Sometimes one fancies that one is in touch with the place where the brightness of consciousness and the darkness of the unconscious intermingle, when one is struggling to remember something one has forgotten. In a peculiar way one feels that consciousness is like an island projecting above the surface of the sea, with the waters of forgetfulness washing lightly against its threshold, sometimes receding and laying bare an inch of land and suggesting that the solid land is not yet at an end. Under the water the island continues—under the threshold of consciousness the same content must exist as in the 'ego', namely something living that also belongs to the soul. For the psyche does not stop where the brightness of consciousness shades off into the darkness of the unconscious. Admittedly, we 'know' nothing of this, but merely feel that the ego is distinct. The ego contains a multiplicity of images and processes which form a unity. Their relation to consciousness acts on them with a kind of gravity impelling them to a centre, the ego, that perceives itself in a way of its own. The ego and consciousness are therefore correlative, each the presupposition of the other. Hence we may say in a purely formal way that a spiritual Something is conscious when it enters into relationship with the ego; where this relationship does not exist, the spiritual Something is unconscious.

But what has become of what has been forgotten? It has been stored up in the palaces of the memory, where all the experiences of the individual life rest for whole decades and longer. And yet they can suddenly come to light again, fill the consciousness often not merely as contents without substance but charged with emotion and challenging the will—exactly as they did so long ago. An object that is in the darkness by accident and is not reached by the searchlight of consciousness has not thereby ceased to exist: it is simply not visible. 'Our unconscious spiritual life exists somewhere or other and very likely it is in no different condition than when it is seen by the ego.'[1] No one has direct knowledge of the unconscious for as soon as it enters consciousness it ceases to be unconscious. All that can be observed and investigated is the influence of the unconscious. Something in the memory that is struggling to come to light can torment us for days on end! The being and nature of the unconscious is just as puzzling as the being of consciousness. It simply 'is'.

How does the act of forgetting take place and under what conditions does something in the conscious mind vanish into the unconscious? Usually it happens by our simply turning our attention to another subject, unreflectingly and unobtrusively. To use a physical image, the content of consciousness loses its 'energetic value'; it is no longer filled with the psychic energy that draws attention to itself like a magnet. Anyone who has to divert his attention from something in order to concentrate on another object, is bound to suppress the previous contents of consciousness, otherwise he cannot in fact change the object of his attention. But normally one can return to the previous object at any time: it can be recalled.

Sometimes, however, it is impossible to forget even when, for some reason or other, a deliberate attempt to forget is made. This inability to forget occurs when an

[1] *Seelenprobleme der Gegenwart*, p. 376.

emotion connected with the content of consciousness releases its energy within us. 'I don't want to think about it any more!' we say. We take up a book or some other activity that requires our whole attention, to distract it from the unpleasant content of consciousness and to resist its claim on our attention. Success varies: the object may no longer be in the consciousness but the emotions connected with it, fear, desire, dissatisfaction remain, though even they can be repressed. There are two ways. Either I can look the fear straight in the face: something inside me is afraid, insecure, I admit it quite frankly; I try not to leave this insecurity unattended— but I know that I want to separate my ego from it, that I want to resist it. I now watch quite calmly to see where the fear makes for. Which of us will win the fight is not yet settled. A silent war is waged within the soul. The emotion is as it were besieged, starved out, and its power gradually dwindles. A natural outlet has been created for the psychic energy. This way requires courage. It is not taken very often since it is more simple to refuse to look at fear, desire, emotion, easier to expel them from oneself with more or less convincing arguments, easier not to recognize them, to say No to reality and to repress them. 'Repression is a kind of semi-conscious and undecided allowing things to drift, or a contempt for grapes that hang too high, or a looking in the other direction to avoid seeing one's own desires.'[1] The feeling and suffering caused by the claims of fear and the other emotions are killed in consciousness. The constantly resisting mood of consciousness keeps the contents down

---

[1] *Psychologie und Religion*, pp. 136ff: 'Suppression, on the other hand, corresponds to a conscious moral decision, whilst repression represents a rather immoral tendency to rid oneself of unpleasant decisions. Suppression can cause distress, conflict and suffering but it never produces a neurosis. Neurosis is always a substitute for legitimate suffering.'

below the threshold of conscious activity. The emotions and contents now below the threshold of consciousness are 'very likely' in the same condition as they were in consciousness, in other words, alive and active. But a content is connected with an emotion—charged with energy—if it has something to say to me, if it concerns me in some way, if it is something I should come to terms with in the brightness of consciousness. This demand which life makes on me must be taken seriously, that is to say, it must either be put into practice, or resistance to its claims must be lived through and suffered honestly. This demand has, however, not been fulfilled but repressed. The life-force or psychic energy has not been taken from the content but buried alive with it, and there below it lives on. Energy cannot be killed, unless the whole individual is to be destroyed; it can only be conveyed to the natural outlet and balanced out. Why indeed should the law of the conservation of energy not apply to psychic energy too?

Repressed contents do not lie dead in this stratum of the unconscious like the triassic formation of the earth. One has only to imagine that the individual tiny creatures of the sediments, ammonites, snails, corals, were still living and interacting, and one has a fair idea of a psyche whose unconscious is filled with repressed contents. In other words, psychic energy, also called libido by Jung, which is repressed with a content of consciousness, continues to act in the unconscious. The repressed and the forgotten form the uppermost stratum of the unconscious.

C. G. Jung has called this stratum the 'personal unconscious'. The contents which have been pushed down below the threshold of consciousness during the lifetime of the individual person constitute the inventory of this psychic space. 'In general, everything that loses an energetic tension, becomes subliminal. If one adds the many subliminal sense perceptions, the many subliminal and semi-subliminal ideas and feelings to the forgotten memories, one gets an idea of what at least the upper layer of the unconscious is made up of.'[1] The process of the formation and accumulation of contents in the unconscious begins in the first moment of human life, in the pre-natal stage. The mother's experiences during pregnancy impress themselves on the unborn child's psyche. The child's consciousness of itself is of course as yet non-existent and only develops gradually in the first years of life: but even the child feels and perceives as a 'whole' person. If pleasure and displeasure, love or pain are given to it or kept from it according to the passing moods and ideas of its teachers, or if pleasant and unpleasant feelings are regulated and adapted to the demands of life: all this does not fail to leave its mark on the small child. The mother will notice the results of the first steps in educating the child not only as they affect its body but its whole nature. It follows that even a child feels as a unity, as a whole person. And this psychic activity takes place only to a very small degree in consciousness. The first experiences of childhood are accompanied by strong feelings and emotions; they make their mark on the psyche, just as footprints may be seen in the snow even when the snow continues to fall. There are in addition two further factors of selection: from within, through slowly awakening abilities and peculiarities of character; from without, through the influence of the environment. The inner or outer world has the stronger influence according to individual character and circumstances. Nature plays an infinitely varied game. The

[1] *Analytische Psychologie und Erziehung*, pp. 61–62.

result is that every child acquires an intimately personal experience of life, and it is this that forms the infantile stratum of the personal unconscious. This in itself explains why the unconscious cannot simply be defined as the antithesis of the conscious. Both are embraced by a greater concept—the psyche. Both are functions and modes of expression of one and the same psychic life. 'From the scientific point of view the Unconscious is no more than a quality of certain psychic phenomena.'[1]

The process of development and precipitation continues. The influences of school, teachers, educators, friends are all experienced at great expense of energy and vital strength. The child's inner world awakens and attempts to map out its own course. We are often amazed to find how entries in diaries or letters reveal how the very things that were once of the deepest spiritual importance to us have vanished from our horizon. Only in this way do we discover how we have developed. The traces left by our development can be seen in externals, in our outward appearance and our technical skills but they make their mark even more in the inner world. The fact that we feel and react involuntarily in this way or that, holding back here, going all out there, suggests that invisible mechanisms have been formed through a long process of time and habit. All this has been observed and taken for granted for a long time, for when human development proceeds in normal circumstances, external as well as internal, the unconscious rests in silence. It is like the quiet surface of the sea, known only by hearsay to those who live far inland. The currents and happenings below the surface of the sea are quite invisible. We notice only indirectly, through a sudden headache, an inexplicable mood or attack of fatigue that there is more

[1] *Analytische Psychologie und Erziehung*, p. 6.

alive and moving within us than we are conscious of. It is not right to ascribe such symptoms to purely physical causes. It is only when the unconscious begins to 'speak' and is induced to abandon its natural mode of existence and invade consciousness that we can discover the laws and relationships with consciousness in accordance with which it is formed. When it invades consciousness it expresses itself in psychic and physical symptoms: slips of the tongue, stuttering, fear, obsessions, fantasies and dreams, pains in particular organs of the body, involuntary actions and all the other symptoms which psychotherapy has reported in the course of time.[1]

In earlier times the causes of such diseases were sought in nervous disturbances, they were regarded as nervous complaints and called 'neuroses'. It was Freud's achievement to introduce and make fruitful in both theory and practice recognition of the psyche as a disease-causing factor.

[1] Cf. the *Psychopathology of Everyday Life* by S. Freud and the text-books of the psychotherapists of every school: O. Schwarz, *Psychogenese und Psychotherapie körperlicher Symptome*, Vienna, 1925; Birnbaum, *Die psychischen Heilmethoden*, Leipzig, 1927; G. R. Heyer, *Organismus der Seele*, Munich, 1932; G. R. Heyer, *Praktische Seelenheilkunde*, Munich, 1933; F. Künkel, *Die Arbeit am Charakter*, Schwerin, 1932; F. Künkel, *Grundzüge der praktischen Seelenheilkunde*, Stuttgart, 1935; I. H. Schultz, *Seelische Krankenbehandlung*, Jena (5th edn.), 1943.

CHAPTER FOUR

NEUROSIS

PSYCHOTHERAPY was confronted with the task of investigating the complicated paths of false psychic development, retracing them, analysing them and penetrating into the depths. A rough survey reveals two main groups of causes of psychic disease: disturbances and false development in sexual life and in social life.

We shall take sexual neurosis first and try to define its frontiers by the roundabout way of analysis. The power neurosis will then reveal the conflict in the inner structure of the psyche and lead us on to the problem of psychological types. This was the way which Jung himself took in order to achieve a synthesis.

It is usual to place the sex instinct next to the instinct of self-preservation from the point of view of its strength and power. The experiences of psychotherapy accord with this order of precedence. They have also demonstrated that the simple instinct of reproduction is not only deeply embedded in the physical but just as deeply rooted in the spiritual nature of man. Two further aspects of the sex instinct must be differentiated. There is on the one hand the purely animal reproductive instinct, sexual desire; but this is permeated, clarified, raised to a different level and 'spiritualized' by the intellectual elements of pleasure in the other person, the need for communion, understanding, tenderness and love. The two aspects are Sexus and Eros. Unfortunately they are hardly ever differentiated in daily life but regarded as one and the same. There is, however, both an interaction and a distinction between the two. Sexus and Eros pass into one another but unbridled lust and passion have nothing in common chemically with the spiritual relationship of love. In marriage Sexus and Eros should interpenetrate and unite the two persons into a supreme communion one with the other. Friendship is dominated by Eros. The inadequate distinction between the two has meant that, in Jung's words, even today we have no sexual morality 'but merely a low barbaric conception based on a completely faulty differentiation. Just as financial business was despised in the Middle Ages, because there was as yet no casuistically differentiated morality of finance but merely an all-inclusive morality, so today we only have an all-inclusive sexual morality'. Lack of understanding has dragged Eros into the mire along with Sexus. 'Past centuries have heaped a burden of moral guilt on Eros.'[1]

It is man's task to fit the sexual instinct into the total pattern of his life. Deviations from the centre bring their revenge: too little *and too much* are both dangerous. An excess of unbridled sexuality leads to emptiness and meaninglessness, disgust with self and disgust with the world and sometimes to obsessional actions such as compulsory washing and the like. But most sexual neuroses show that too little scope has been given to the sexual instinct. In many cases the varied manifestations of sexual neurosis, usually those which the minister of religion comes across, can be traced back to a common root. The basic trouble is that the sexual instinct has been regarded as something evil, inferior, criminal, unworthy of a 'decent' human being. And this attitude is applied not only to the purely physical side but to all knowledge of sex and especially everything connected

[1] *Das Unbewusste im normalen und kranken Seelenleben*, pp. 30 and 43.

with marriage. The milder form of neurosis is reconciled to a passive toleration of sex as something 'one does not talk about', but it still has a more or less bad conscience about it. Sometimes this attitude has become so much part of a person's everyday outlook on life that it is held quite unconsciously. Insecurity and fear of these things are all that remains; sexual matters are regarded as criminal and sinful. Whatever is wicked must be expelled from the soul, by force if necessary—and thus from the very outset all stirrings of Eros and Sexus are suppressed, killed off, or so one imagines. But the psychologist calls the process repression. A conscious attitude of resistance persisting through many years keeps these 'sinful' contents below the threshold of consciousness, but only artificially. An instinct cannot be killed; it lives on in the unconscious. It is like a farmer in whose meadow a spring rises, which he stops up so as not to lose any of his meadowland. For a time all appears to be well, but in the meantime the water has in fact hollowed out the whole soil, for it is bound to seek an outlet and in the end it forces its way to the surface and lays the whole meadow waste.

The results of a wrong attitude to sex show themselves when sometime or other the sexual instinct breaks through, directly, by inundating the psyche with sexuality or, indirectly, in the form of a neurosis. This may take the form of some tiny, hardly perceptible idiosyncrasy or it may lead to a serious 'disease of the soul'. It is sad that the number of such patients who come from religious establishments, or whose education has been strongly marked by religious influences, is very considerable.

What is a neurosis, according to Jung? 'The teleological purpose of neurosis is an attempt to cure itself on the part of the psyche.'[1] Just as fever and inflammation are reactions of the organism. A neurosis is not merely a danger signal, like pain, it is more than that: it is an attempt at self-help, a resolve to take a definite line and a definite direction. All psychic processes are directed towards a certain tendency but this has become jammed up, as in a dead end which blocks up consciousness. And raging against the symptom only makes the conflict worse. The patient is like a man who has fallen into a river and is sinking; but the psychotherapist challenges him to act like a diver. For the place where the patient suffers is not accidental; it conceals buried treasure which only a diver can raise. The patient is everything in one and the same person: the water, the man who has fallen in the water, the treasure and the diver. The treasure lies in his soul, it is part of him. Through ignorance or through being misinformed he has treated it so badly that it has sunk, gone down below the waves and become cut off from consciousness. The whole complex of the sexual is thus excluded from consciousness and becomes autonomous, obeying its own laws. It enters into unconscious opposition to the outlook of consciousness and insists on going its own way. It expresses itself in the desire for healing. But the way to a cure is obstructed by the attitude of the ego. Thus neurosis can also be defined as an inner schism, a dissension within. The treasure in the unconscious is waiting to be raised. The tangle of its contents must be taken up by consciousness, slowly unravelled and rejoined to consciousness again. This is the formal process of healing. The disease has become a pointer to spiritual recovery in general. 'The new way of thinking about oneself bears no more resemblance to the previous state of mind than the diver bears to the

[1] *Versuch einer Darstellung der psychoanalytischen Theorie*, p. 400.

drowning man.' Neurosis therefore has a dual aspect;
negatively it is an evil, a disease; but positively it draws
attention to a sore spot in the psyche, it is a guide to
recovery, it is itself already part of the way to recovery
because it points to the seat of the disease. Its meaning
and purpose are that it draws our attention to a place
where an unlived part of our nature lies buried, so that
we are able to take up the separated part of the soul—the
'divided part of the soul'—and become a whole person.
All the energies, abilities and tendencies of the personality must be taken up into the experience and the
suffering, must be developed and organized quite consciously, for it is only then that man is what he is intended
to be by nature. This is the way to the development of
personality: the psyche must attain to a full knowledge
and activation of its gifts.

It follows that the imperative requirement for physical
and spiritual health is to take up all the energies and
abilities of the psyche into experience. An unlived part
of the psyche acts like a bacillus or a foreign body, like an
ulcer or poison. But what is meant by 'unlived' and
'living'? Does it mean that every impulse of a sexual
nature must be freely indulged in? 'Psychoanalysis has
been criticized for liberating the (fortunately) repressed
animal instincts and impulses of man and thereby
causing untold disaster. . . . It is quite true that analysis
liberates the animal instincts, but not, as some understand it, in order to abandon them to unbridled exploita-
tion but to make them available for higher uses, as far as
this is possible for particular individuals and as far as
such (sublimated) use can be achieved.'[1] The difference
between giving life to an impulse and giving it free rein
is like the difference between twilight and the full night

[1] *Das Unbewusste im normalen und kranken Seelenleben*, p. 40.

or day. No one can see where this intermediate stage leads to, it trembles undecided in the balance, it makes decision possible. But it exists in light and darkness at the same time. The autonomous complex, in this case, the sexual complex, has to be led into this state of suspension, out of the night of the unconscious into the slowly self-absorbing light of consciousness. In the intermediary stage man feels the pulsation of life, and if he has no fear and does not run away he can pass the possibilities of life quietly in review before his mind's eye and make a decision in perfect tranquillity. He can turn to the light, allow its rays to penetrate his spirit more and more and submit to reason. The slow transition from the darkness to the light has the important result that life invades the brightness of the intellect and abstract, 'sterilized' and barren concepts can no longer construct a skeleton in deadly silence—like a dry commentary on the poetry of life. The mind lowers itself as it were and seeks to enter into relation with the basic energies of the psyche, the impulses and instincts, and the marriage takes place in that chiaroscuro where consciousness and the unconscious meet and pass over into one another. But the symbol passes over the bridge as mediator, charged with life and energy which are now available to consciousness for new tasks.

In this way, the sore spot, in this case, the sexual problem, loses its actuality. But, more than that, when the patient has fully recovered, a quietness of mind sets in, a calm delight in the fact of sexuality; in other words, the fulfilment of sexual desire is subordinate to conscious decision. The ego has become master of it, it (the ego) has enlarged its sovereign territory. A new province has been conquered and the ego can now make use of the treasures of this new kingdom. This is a step nearer to completeness of personality and self-mastery. The schism

between ego and instinct, their dissension, has been
annulled by the entry of both into a higher unity. The
ego has had to alter its view of sexual processes in favour
of an attitude that unites and embraces both partners:
consciousness and the unconscious. The deprecatory
attitude of consciousness and the demand for life of the
instincts, which springs from the depths of the unconscious, were formerly two contradictory tendencies of the
soul. But now they are reconciled; a natural balance
has restored its rights to the formerly imprisoned and
dammed-up energies. The other spheres and tasks of life
now seem important again: they too had been obstructed.
This process is basically different from Freud's sublimation of the instincts. Freud asserts that the sexual and
indeed only basic energy of the soul (psychosexuality) is
altered, clarified, 'diluted', de-sexualized and sublimated, so that culture emerges from sublimation.
'This is a psychology of the ramifications of the sexual
instinct in the human soul.'[1] In Jung's conception of the
soul sex is one impulse, one gift, one sphere of life among
many others. But it is there that the state of war has
concentrated all the powers and energies of life which
can only become free and break the blockade when the
neurosis is resolved. Then they can flow again into other
spheres of life, revive them and reactivate them. They
suddenly appear important again to the ego, they present
it with a new task. The process is reflected in consciousness but not in the sense that the neurosis is solved like
a problem in algebra: psychic problems are not solved
but 'grown out of and beyond'.

This is the theory of the healing process; in practice the
process develops in infinitely varied ways in the doctor's
consulting room during the analysis.

---

[1] *Analytische Psychologie und Erziehung*, p. 32.

CHAPTER FIVE

THE ANALYSIS

THE patient goes to the nerve doctor to seek a cure for his disease and suddenly finds himself involved in a personal conversation. It is clear that this situation, if it is to be successful, makes demands on both sides which go deeper and involve greater responsibilities than is usual in the relationship between the doctor and the physically sick. Not only the physical sphere is entrusted to the doctor, a complete stranger, but the spiritual sphere is also exposed to his influence. If many people find it difficult to strip their bodies naked before a stranger, then the sense of shame will be even more acute when they are confronted with questions intended to penetrate the most intimate places of the soul: and this is absolutely necessary in psychotherapy.

Only the personality of the doctor who immediately takes upon himself the patient's suffering and gives it a place in his sympathy and affection, can bring relief. This response of affection quickly creates a common ground. With the constant flow of patients in and out of the consulting room it is not always easy for the doctor to respond to the calls on his sympathy. But a merely scientific interest in a case freezes up a spiritual relationship which can only thrive in the warmth of mutual kindness. It is difficult, even with the best will in the world, to sympathize with all human types. Some are bound to be inherently alien; their nature awakens no response, they are tuned in to different wavelengths. This

severely limits the possibilities of therapeutic treatment.
The doctor who reacts negatively to such patients cannot
deal with them at all. For unless both sides are inwardly
prepared for the dialectical process of analysis which is
'an interaction of one psychic system (that of the patient)
with another (that of the doctor)' it is impossible for the
atmosphere to be formed in which a spiritual disease such
as a neurosis can be brought to an end. But the more
mature the doctor is as a human being the more he will
be able to cope with the most varied types of patient.

C. G. Jung once issued a questionnaire to educated
Protestants and Catholics asking to whom they preferred
to turn when they were in spiritual trouble, the priest or
the doctor? Of the Protestants 57 per cent. voted for the
doctor, of the Catholics only 24 per cent. Among the
arguments brought against the priest were lack of
psychological knowledge and understanding, preconceived opinions, dogmatic and traditional bigotry.[1] The
question is, what will my priest think of me if I tell him
about the day-dreams which torment me, or even begin
to tell him about the embarrassments in which my dis-
ordered instincts involve me? All he will see is the conflict
of these situations with his own morality, and he will
classify me accordingly without making any attempt to
understand me. Doubt upon doubt haunts me in religious
matters and the traditional religious set-up leaves me
cold. The priest will condemn me even though he may
not actually say so. These are the sort of misgivings that
are expressed against consulting the priest. One must
admit, however, that the doctor is watched no less
anxiously to see if he will condemn the patient. Jung
infers from this that 'there is no contact between doctor
and patient if the doctor condemns; whether he does so

[1] *Die Beziehungen der Psychotherapie zur Seelsorge*, pp. 13ff.

verbally or silently makes no difference to the effect'. Contact with the inner soul of the patient which gives access to the invisibly bleeding wounds and enables the doctor to minister to the quiet processes of the soul, comes about only through 'unprejudiced objectivity'. Without prejudice, without fear of moral and dogmatic facts the 'healer' must ascertain the facts of the case purely objectively. The patient wants to feel that the very things about himself which alarm him most are simply accepted by the doctor as sheer facts. This does not mean that he wants the doctor to take them for granted: that would be just as bad as condemning them. Acceptance of the facts of the case is not a matter of mere words either, it is rather 'something human, something like respect for the facts, for the human being suffering from the facts, respect for the mystery of this particular human life. Such is the attitude of the truly religious man. He knows that God has created all kinds of strange incomprehensible things and seeks to reach the human heart by the strangest possible ways. Hence he senses in all things the dark presence of the divine will. This is what I mean by an attitude of unprejudiced objectivity. It is the moral achievement of the doctor who must not be disgusted by disease and putrefaction. It is impossible to change anything one does not first accept.'[1] This attitude presupposes that the therapist has at some time or other experienced in himself the kind of things that can arise from the human heart. He must have been through the analytical process in himself and 'have looked behind the scenes of his own psyche with the help of modern psychology'. This will have shown him how difficult it is to accept everything, to 'accept' himself and regard himself as a natural product in the raw state. He must

[1] *loc. cit.*, p. 18.

have come up against the fact that the vice of the pious is bad temper and he must have observed the automatic transformation of the angel of the streets and church into the termagent, to undermine his false sense of security and self-confidence. Ideas, purposes, feelings and aims are only the superficial, visible froth above the autonomous surge and sweep of life. To take a look behind the scenes of one's own mind and spirit in this way is frightening: it is an encounter with the innermost human being, with his 'shadow', as Jung says, from which there is no escape. The therapist must have been through this dark portal in order to know how relative the foreground of man's spiritual life really is: and this again is not a matter of intellectual ability, but experience. Consciousness is like a tiny ship tossed about by the waves of the sea. The boards of the ship are made of the particular conventions of the age: fashion, tradition, public opinion. In neurosis the ship has sprung a leak. Anyone who now becomes depressed and alarmed by the dark inventory in the inner soul is like a sailor whose main concern is to find out what the water that is invading his ship is made of instead of stopping up the leak. The dark misery of man must be seen in just the same way as the daylight of the soul and the lofty qualities of the spirit. 'In reality the acceptance of the dark side of the soul is something verging on the impossible. Think what it means to acknowledge the right to exist of the irrational, the senseless and the evil. But that is precisely what modern man wants to do: he wants to live with what he is; he wants to know what he is.'[1] The traversing of the shadow is the presupposition of the right psychotherapeutic approach, the approach of unprejudiced objectivity. It is infinitely more important than psychological

[1] *loc. cit.*, p. 23.

theories and methods and makes the patient feel that he is being understood; it also prevents him feeling that he is being docketed and classified. This attitude of un-prejudiced objectivity is like a wireless set which can be tuned in to all wavelengths. It accepts everything and excludes no single possibility in the total fullness of life, thus avoiding the onesidedness of all particular schools. 'One must not know or imagine one knows what is right and what is wrong, otherwise something of the richness of life will be excluded; one must rather keep one's eye exclusively on that which actually happens—and only that which acts, is actual.'[1]

The realities in the patient's spiritual life are the material to which analysis has to be applied. The analysis comes into ever closer touch with the patient's psychic life as the therapist's medicine gently takes effect; it is a dialectical process that takes place step by step, between the patient and the analyst. But in view of all that has been said about unprejudiced objectivity this means to begin with that the diagnosis must be taken positively rather than negatively, as a desire to be healed on the part of the soul. The process must 'go the same way as the illness itself, the wrong way, the way that sharpens the conflicts and increases the loneliness until it grows unbearable—in the hope that from the psychic depths from which all destruction comes, there may also grow the powers of salvation'.[2]

On looking at a crucifix a woman is sexually excited. Visions arise which her strictly religious conscience finds unbearable. The doctor instructs her to hold a crucifix in front of her daily and look at it. The woman looks up at the doctor, in alarm. Surely looking at the crucifix every day will mean summoning the visions, causing the

[1] *loc. cit.*, p. 24.   [2] *loc. cit.*, p. 26.

very temptations she is so anxious to avoid! Sometimes
patients do not believe the doctor when he tells them
that ordinary standards do not apply to them because
their soul is sick (a condition to be strictly differentiated
from mental disease). It is good if the doctor can find a
priest to help him in such cases, a priest who will undertake the unburdening of the conscience and it is good if
in response to the priestly word the obstruction in the way
of recovery is removed. With the barrier removed the way
of sickness can be trod and the soul's 'desire' be fulfilled,
that is, the desire to give the sexual its rightful place.

Another very religious woman is plagued by an
incessant fear of rape. Every contact with pictures of the
human body, every reference to sex and love that she
must make in her capacity as a professional teacher takes
hold of her. imagination and occupies her mind excessively and for unnaturally long periods at a time. Calm
consideration shows that the actual likelihood of rape is
extremely remote but the inexplicable fear continues to
whisper incessantly in her soul. Anamnesis reveals a
characteristically false and narrow education with
repressions from childhood onwards. This otherwise
lively young woman had never dared to think out the
natural process between man and woman in love and
marriage since it was, as she imagined, ugly and sinful.
The spheres of Sexus and Eros had not been assimilated
by the ego but deliberately withdrawn and repressed.
In the darkness of the unconscious Sexus and Eros gave
out sultry fumes and dammed up the sexual energy. The
tension thus created was unable to find a natural outlet
and harboured destructive possibilities like a crater, a
flood or an explosion. Of this the woman was rightly
afraid—but the cause was hidden in her own soul—it
did not come from outside her at all.

In both cases something external was held responsible whereas the real cause lay in the subject herself. The effects of the complexes lying within the unconscious were projected outwards. What has to be done in such cases is to detach the projection from the object and make clear to the patient that the sexual visions and the fear only come from the incalculable and unknown forces in her own soul. The patient's horror at her own wickedness must be balanced by a simultaneous enlightenment worked out gradually in the course of several consultations.

Sexual life in the psyche needs space, space permeated and cultivated by experience. The other spheres of life must also be worked through in a process of hard training, for instance professional training. If this task is neglected and consciousness attaches no importance to it, the scale on the other side of the balance will sink all the deeper, in the literal as well as the metaphorical sense. 'The psyche seems like a balance, the beam of which lies partly in the unconscious, partly in the conscious. If it rises on the conscious side by an intensification of conscious functions (for example, repression) the other part sinks all the more deeply into the unconscious and produces reactions there.'[1] Now it is also possible to express the relationship between the conscious and the unconscious in a law which Jung calls a 'categorical presupposition': consciousness and the unconscious stand to one another in the relationship of balance or 'compensation'. Consciousness and the unconscious are two aspects of the one psyche which is a heterogeneous continuum; there is a 'complementary correlation' between them. Every action on the one side is related to

[1] A. Keller, *Analytische Psychologie und Religionsforschung*, in *Jung-Festschrift*, Berlin, 1935, p. 289.

happenings on the other side. 'The activity of the conscious is *selective*. Selection demands *direction*. But direction requires the *exclusion of everything irrelevant*. On occasion, therefore, a certain one-sidedness of the conscious orientation is inevitable. The contents that are excluded and inhibited by the chosen direction sink into the unconscious, where by virtue of their effective existence they form a definite counterweight against the conscious orientation.'[1] The contents of the personal unconscious correspond to the same kind of contents in the conscious. In this stratum of the psychic structure the unconscious can be explained by the conscious and vice versa: each is the proof of the other's existence. A false approach to the sexual points to the existence of repressed contents in the unconscious. Typical projections of the unconscious (as in the cases described above) suggest the diagnosis of a wrongly directed sexual education and an unnatural attitude to sex.

The consequences of the law of compensation for education and psychology are important. Every evasion, every prudish attitude is avenged in a reaction of some kind, whether it takes the form of a vague feeling of insecurity, fear or neurotic substitute actions and projections. Every unnatural action is compensated for by unnaturalness, that is to say, by an excessive swing to the opposite side, which may take the form of psychic suffering and illness in serious cases. Every compensation is an attempt to create a balance, which is why neurosis may be defined as 'the soul's desire for healing'.

The explanation given to the patient will run something like that. But it is up to the patient to make the new knowledge his own. A great part of psychotherapeutic

[1] *Psychologische Typen*, p. 606 (English: p. 532). In this passage Jung also points out that the term 'compensation' comes from Adler.

activity consists in helping to meet all the evasions and leading the patient to the goal over and over again: helping him to change his attitude to the sexual and thereby release the contents of the unconscious. As soon as it is set free the dammed up sexuality will shrink to normal proportions. The tension between consciousness and the unconscious disappears and the renewed activity of self-regulating compensation is guaranteed by their mutual approach. In normal cases compensation by the unconscious is not in contrast to but a completion of the conscious orientation, which takes place unconsciously; it has an unconscious regulating effect on the activities of consciousness. Compensation is a functional harmonizing and self-regulating of the 'psychic apparatus'.

Midway between complete unconsciousness of the compensatory processes and opposition to them in neurosis there is a condition of tension of great significance for analysis and psychological research in general. 'This tension involves a certain inhibition of the conscious activity which can assuredly be broken down by increased conscious effort. But as time goes on, the tension becomes so acute that the inhibited unconscious contents begin to break through into consciousness in the form of dreams and spontaneous images.'[1] They are the bridge into the depths of the soul.

[1] *Psychologische Typen*, p. 607 (English: pp. 532–3).

CHAPTER SIX

DREAMS

D REAMS and fantasies, so-called day-dreams, rising from the unconscious are part of everyone's experience. From the very beginning humanity has taken an interest in these strange phenomena in the soul; interpretation of dreams has been universal. Until our own time, however, science has avoided this uncertain and fluctuating field. It had no methods or concepts by which to explain dreams and fantasies.

Once again the sufferings of the spiritually sick made a closer investigation of dreams and fantasies imperative. The working hypothesis of the unconscious provided the spiritual background, the source from which dreams and fantasies flow. Thus dream-analysis became the 'royal bridge'[1] into the unconscious. In dreams the unconscious speaks: they are its direct expression. They are removed from the censoring influence of consciousness and represent an involuntary reality of the soul. The dream is a natural product of the psyche. It brings to light repressed elements, desires and fears, moral indifference, but also all the infantile, perverse and criminal tendencies of the soul. According to Freud, the unconscious is a wastepaper basket of spiritual refuse and dreams a demonic monster. 'It is to be noted that the dreams of people whose actions are morally beyond reproach bring to light materials that must be called immoral in the normal sense of the term. Thus it is characteristic that St. Augustine was glad not to have to account to God

[1] The expression derives from S. Freud.

for his dreams.'[1] Moral indignation at this discovery .is merely a token of a fear of nature and reality. Rightly understood, the unconscious is 'a morally, aesthetically and intellectually indifferent natural being that becomes dangerous only when our conscious attitude to it is hopelessly wrong'. According to Jung the unconscious is not merely the result of repression. Conscious and unconscious are bound up with one another by the law of compensation which is expressed in the strictest form of causality imaginable and in a most delicately poised state of balance. 'In dreams, for instance, the unconscious may supply all those contents which are constellated by the conscious situation, but which are inhibited by conscious selection, although a knowledge of them would be quite indispensable to a complete adaptation.'[2]

To discover the meaning of dreams we must therefore ask not merely such questions as why, for what reasons does the unconscious tell me this, what is at fault, where is the hidden wound? Such questions are the key to many interpretations but not all. The unconscious stands in correlation and therefore has something to say of its own account. To take the question a stage further we must ask what is the purpose of the unconscious, what kind of a hint is it trying to give, which of our conscious attitudes is so one-sided that it needs to be compensated by the unconscious? The dream is a message from the unconscious in the veiled language of symbols. The purpose of the contents of the dream cannot be seen from outside; first of all analysis is needed to reach the real compensatory factors of the hidden content. 'Most of the defensive reactions of the body, the purpose of which has

[1] *Über die Energetik der Seele*, p. 125.
[2] *Psychologische Typen*, p. 607 (English: p. 533).

only been recognized as a result of deeper experience and detailed examination, are of this hidden, indirect nature. I merely recall here the significance of fever and the suppuration of an infected wound.'[1] The workmanlike rule for the interpretation of dreams is therefore: 'What conscious attitude is compensated for by the dream?' In this way the dream fulfils, even in the normal life of the soul, the function of an organ of information and control and can serve as an effective aid in building up the personality. How important dreams and sleep can therefore become for spiritual development! Man spends almost half his life in a more or less unconscious state.

The contents of dreams can be unfulfilled wishes and fears (thus far Freud), inexorable truths, philosophical theses, illusions, wild fantasies, memories, plans, anticipations, telepathic visions, irrational experiences, etc. From this we may propound two hypotheses for their interpretation:

1. 'Every dream has a meaning.' This is not disproved by the difficulty of understanding what the meaning is, for the interpretation of dreams is still in its very earliest stages. The mentality accustomed to abstract modes of thinking has first to familiarize itself with the alogical imagery of the dream world. Dreams resist the stranglehold of cause and effect. They are based not on the logical proximity but on an interweaving of events. The Western mode of thought has much to learn from the Oriental in this respect.

2. 'Dreams have something essential to add to conscious knowledge.' This means that every dream is relative to the particular situation in which the conscious mind finds itself. And this makes any universally valid interpretation of dreams quite out of the question. A

[1] *Über die Energetik der Seele*, p. 139.

dream can be interpreted only on the basis of full knowledge of the concomitant condition of consciousness. Even symbols, of which Freud compiled a catalogue, stand for different things in different dreams. Jung, who deals with 1,500 to 2,000 dreams a year, takes as his presuppositions: 'do not try to impose a meaning on the dream' and 'uncertainty is the only certainty'. The main difficulty in interpreting dreams, however, is that although all dreams are related to the contents of consciousness by the law of compensation, the compensatory function is often very difficult to ascertain; although the dream contributes to the psychological direction of the self by bringing up automatically everything that has been repressed and neglected and ignored, its compensatory significance is often not clear 'because our knowledge of the nature and needs of the human soul is still incomplete'.[1]

This brings us to a consequence which follows from the relationship between consciousness and the contents of the unconscious which we have expounded. Since both are correlative the unconscious acquires a quite unsuspected significance; from the standpoint of the whole direction of life it stands equal in value alongside the conscious; of equal value, not higher in value, as was thought in the first enthusiasm of discovery. 'In my opinion, which is based on numerous enquiries over many years, the importance of the unconscious for the total achievement of the psyche is probably just as great as that of consciousness.'[2] The needs of the soul arise from both sources. The essential nature of a soul is only revealed when both are attended to. Where is the resultant between them? What is their common goal and

[1] *Über die Energetik der Seele*, pp. 133-134.
[2] *loc. cit.*, p. 141.

which way guarantees the health of the soul? The way that depth-psychology has taken so far has made us uncertain and thrown overboard the preconceived notion that all these things are established truths.

To sum up: this is the way that results from all this for analysis: the establishing of the condition of consciousness is followed by borings into the unconscious; neurotic symptoms and dreams provide hints which can be interpreted on the basis of the law of compensation. The material brought to light has hitherto been excluded from consciousness and 'transcendent' to it; it must be attached to it and assimilated by it. Jung calls this process the 'Transcendent Function'. The making conscious of and the grappling with the contents and the living through them that this makes necessary are stages. Through the assimilation of unconscious contents the conscious life which deviates from the path of health is assimilated to it again and led to its natural autonomy. Consciousness extends its sphere and the sense of consciousness is heightened. What was merely drifting about in the unconscious is made accessible to the care and directive purpose of the conscious ego. The assimilated and cultivated spheres of life are therefore naturally finer, higher, more differentiated and more human. Translated into sexual terms this means that Sexus and Eros are open to more refined forms of love and affection; animal lust is developed into human love.

CHAPTER SEVEN

THE PROBLEM OF TYPES

U P till now we have been dealing above all with the sexual neurosis which produces conflicts and collisions with the inner psychic world. People who suffer from sexual neurosis are so conditioned by the object and live so 'externally' that faulty adaptation to the inner world evokes conflicts. It is the error of Freud and his school to classify and judge all men according to this schema. Adler swings over to the opposite extreme. Jung has taught us to understand the antitheses between the two schools. We propose to follow his line of enquiry and contrast sexual neurosis with power neurosis.

There are neuroses of which the symptoms are exactly like those of sexual neurosis but which do not yield to the treatment we have discussed. When the condition of consciousness is examined it reveals no sexual repression of any kind and yet such patients are pursued by sexual fantasies or constant headaches which hinder study, or a morbid dread of public places (agorophobia) which makes professional progress difficult, or a paralysis which cripples all activity. In all these cases there is no evidence of any organic trouble and yet the sufferings are as real and active as in an organic disease. In analysis the symptoms yield to no search for an unconscious cause for they are a means to an end, the means of expression of an aspiration. But purpose and aspiration—like Freud's 'cause'—are hidden and unconscious; yet they influence the patient's position in the community very considerably. For instance he may be prevented from finishing his studies by headaches—in order to escape the responsibility of a profession; or a member of a family may draw the attention of the whole family to himself by a paralysis—in order not to have to submit to a more highly gifted sister.

Adler pointed to the powers working in the background and classified them as the ego and the community. By so doing he opened up new perspectives for analysis. On the one side there is the ego with its striving for position, self-expression and moulding the outside world in accordance with its own plans; on the other side there is the requirement of the community that the individual shall subordinate himself to the Whole. A wrong solution of the problem that this antithesis between the ego and the community presents leads to a conflict with the world around us.

The tension is between the sense of personality (the experience of the ego) and the just as innate sense of community. The sense of personality feels inferior when confronted with some particular situation in life but the ego lacks the courage or is too ambitious to admit the feeling and consequently it is repressed. In this way the psyche is constantly forced to install safety devices in the form of over-compensations, so that the sense of inferiority does not get the upper hand; if necessary unconsciously by means of physical symptoms such as we have touched on above. Every action is then determined by this unconscious security measure which has a hypnotic effect on the whole life of the psyche.

The relations to the community of such people are always seen through the coloured spectacles of their own ego. They do not acquiesce in the resultant between the ego and the community. Their spiritual life has become reduced to the polarity between society and self, not, as in the case of sexual neurosis, instinct and intellect. Many people belong to this type of reaction.

The vengeance which the unconscious takes is what Adler calls the 'power neurosis'. Whilst in Freud's view the repression must be annulled if a cure is to take place, what has to be annulled here is the isolating safety device. Many people can also be helped by being made conscious of their hidden line of security and superiority which enables them to adapt themselves to the demands of life.

But there is no reason why everyone should have health-endangering difficulties here. Every child has sometimes had difficulty in obeying and has wanted to have its own way. But many children train themselves in time to accept the middle way and find the balance between justifiable claims and concessions to family life without inflicting any sort of wound on their sense of personality. Their character can therefore never be revealed by individual psychology. On the other hand, there are many children who do not survive the battle of adaptation and subordination to society without damage to their personalities: they are built differently, they react differently; this is their sensitive side. They live more inwardly, their ego is more accentuated than their sense of community. They are a more subjective type.

If one compares the Freudian and Adlerian conception of man one turns out to be the negative of the other. 'They are the contrast between the two types of human mentality: the one derives its determining influence predominantly from the subject, the other from the object.'[1] Nature herself has produced various types and bred various differences of temperament. Jung now takes a step forward. He introduces the natural differences between human types into his enquiry without exaggerating any particular one. He has taken the two most

[1] *Das Unbewusste im normalen und kranken Seelenleben*, p. 63.

prevalent forms of neurosis, sexual neurosis and power neurosis, as the basis for his discussion of the problem of human types.

He asks: 'How does it come about that one enquirer sees only the one side, and another enquirer only the other? And why do both of them imagine theirs is the only valid view? It probably arises from the fact that both, according to their own particular psychological temperament, see in neurosis precisely that which corresponds to their own character.'[1] Freud and Adler transferred their own particular temperament to all others and explained their fellow men on the basis of their own psychology. They widened their neuropathic methods, which were so successful in many individual cases, into a general psychological conception, so that both theories are the product of a one-sided attitude. The 'Freudian man' is conditioned by the object; all this energy is directed outwards, he is ' extroverted'. The antithesis of this is the Adlerian type who is determined by the subject. All his energy is concentrated on the ego and turned inwards. Jung calls him the 'introverted type'. Jung interprets them both as different varieties of man. He reconciles the antithesis between them in a higher unity. The reality of the psyche is split up into the opposite poles of subject and object. The different valuation accorded to them and the tension between them results in different spiritual attitudes, the so-called types. Jung sees Freud and Adler as themselves well-pronounced representatives of the two types. Freud is an extravert and Adler an introvert. But their doctrines are not general theories about the human soul but descriptions of the two types. Jung describes their methods as 'corrosives for the doctor's hand, to be used locally' for

[1] *loc. cit.*, p. 91.

they are 'reductive and destructive'. Inversely, the patient requires the method best suited to his type.

Jung pursued the problem of types by studying the great personalities of history and distinguishing between two opposing types. They are clearly defined in the persons of Plato and Aristotle. Plato constructs his world from his own mind; he is an introvert, whereas it is the clarity of the object that is evident in all Aristotle's definitions: he represents the extrovert type. Both accord with two trends which run through the history of the human mind from Classical times and the Middle Ages right into our own age (considered from the psychological, not the epistemological angle). The antithesis is repeated in St. Augustine and St. Thomas. Nominalism is Platonic; realism is its reverse. They are continued and reach their logical conclusion in rationalism and materialism. The Idea and the Thing fall more and more apart. The course of the history of the human mind in Europe mirrors the development of the soul of Western man. The division of Idea and Thing leads to two blind alleys: the subjective accentuation of the ego and the complete isolation of the rational solipsist, of the neurotic power addict (Nietzsche!) and the surrender and total abandonment to the object in the person of the sensualist and the practical materialist of the Freudian type.

In the realm of art Jung opposes the Apollinian type (introvert) to the Dionysian (extrovert). Goethe and Schiller are examples of the two types. Schiller himself worked out a theory of types corresponding to Jung's theory of introversion and extroversion. In poetry the intellectual character of the two friends is reflected in their 'sentimental' and 'naïve' poetry. Schiller 'searches for nature', he is an idealist; Goethe is himself nature, he is a realist. The two antipodes of Nietzsche and Wagner are likewise representative of the two types, each almost excessively intense, hard and lonely. Nietzsche wanted to turn the world upside down and rebuild it according to his own ideas; Wagner imprisoned all the desires of the world in his music. In the 700 pages of his book on the problem of types Jung certainly proves the fruitfulness of his terminology (intro- and extro-version).

The first aspect that requires discussion in a general description of the two types is the different relationship of the subject to the object. It is either positive or negative. The introvert lives in the subject: 'the subject is the centre of all his interests'. The ego is his familiar ground. He is suspicious of the object, he is reserved and hesitant in his relationship to the external world. But when he becomes active, everything must go according to his plans even if they do not happen to suit the particular situation. The extrovert vivifies the particular spheres of his soul which are in touch with the outside world. 'The object acts like a magnet on the tendencies of the subject.' He is open and helpful to the outside world, he is easy to influence, he adapts himself to every situation, he makes contacts easily—he lives outwards. His weakness and limitation is mere 'adaptation, without creative re-formation'. Both the introvert and the extrovert have their strength and their value, but also their weakness. 'What is worth while to the one is worthless to the other.' They supplement one another in the struggle of life and are fond of marrying one another; they attract one another and each admires in the other what he lacks himself. In marriage they stand back to back and protect one another when troubles come.

The introvert and extrovert types are universal, fundamental attitudes to life. They are 'the central switchboard from which on the one hand external actions are regulated and on the other hand specific experience is moulded'.[1] But what is in fact switched over? The difference of the introverts among themselves and among the extroverts too are so great that the question is inevitable. Jung's book on psychological types is the fruit of nearly ten years' effort to answer the question.

Jung takes the different psychological functions as criteria of the differences within the basic attitudes. These crystallize out into two pairs: thinking and feeling; sensation and intuition. The first two are rational, the other two irrational. Jung is open to contradiction on the justification of this terminology and classification: 'Psychology is terra nova in which the terminology has still to be established. It is well known that temperatures can be measured according to Réaumur, Celcius or Fahrenheit: one merely has to state which scale one has used.' 'Everyone except the philosophers knows what is meant by thinking.' But feeling requires closer explanation, particularly as it is considered 'rational'. Jung singles out one meaning from the various meanings of 'feeling'. The feeling of regret is a judgement arising from the depths of the intellect. It expresses a feeling logically and clearly, expressing judgement exactly in the same way as thinking. The function of feeling shares this rationality with the function of thinking. Both make judgements and valuations. In this they are sharply divided from sensation and intuition or premonition. They perceive, they are perceptions. Sensation is fed by conscious sense experience, intuition by unconscious sense experience, which is why they are often called feeling, a habit Jung would like to see completely abolished. Sensation and intuition perceive occurrences, but do not judge and evaluate them like

[1] *Seelenprobleme der Gegenwart*, p. 132.

their two antipodes. They are only open to the actual happening, to what is taking place.

These four functions or spiritual energies provide something in the nature of a complete guide to the spiritual sphere, like the four points of the compass in the geographical sphere. 'Sensation establishes what is actually present. Thinking makes it possible for us to perceive the meaning of what is actually present and feeling, what it is worth. Finally, intuition points to the possibilities of whence and whither which are latent in what is actually occurring at present.'[1]

Jung concedes to his critics that the cardinal points in the spiritual sphere can be shifted by as many degrees as one likes and can even be given different names. He regards that as merely a matter of convention and intelligibility. But he has found that they provide him with an adequate system of measurement and orientation on his voyages of psychological discovery.

Now all four functions can occur in the two basic attitudes. Hence eight variants are possible. The most highly developed function impresses its stamp on a man, it is the expression of his personality, its purpose, desire, achievement. For example, there is an introverted type of thinking, an extroverted type of feeling, and so on. But what about the other functions and capacities? They are equally present in every human being. 'Accurate investigation of the individual case consistently reveals the fact that, in conjunction with the most differentiated function, another function of secondary importance, and therefore of inferior differentiation in consciousness is constantly present and is a relatively determining factor.'[2] The two missing functions in the

[1] *Seelenprobleme der Gegenwart*, p. 143.
[2] *Psychologische Typen*, pp. 58off (English: 513).

totality are not fully developed but still unconscious. They belong to the opposite type of attitude. From this it is obvious which variations and mixtures can occur. For all that, the conceptually intelligible functions are only 'family photographs which cumulate the common and at the same time typical characteristics and therefore give them undue emphasis, whilst the individual characteristics are unduly blurred'. At this point Jung takes a step which takes us further, not so much into a wider exposition as into the depths of the psyche. Any kind of event can bring the inferior and unconscious function to the top and this is expressed in irritability. But this is again a symptom of an already existing inferiority. It results in the possibility of dissension and misunderstanding, not only the dissension of two people but also dissension within the individual. 'The nature of the inferior function is characterized by autonomy: it is independent, it attacks us, it fascinates us and absorbs us so that we are no longer master of ourselves and no longer share justly between ourselves and the others.'[1] If man and wife fight against trouble back to back, if they succeed in safeguarding their marriage, their family and life's work and if the husband has earned enough money—they get time to occupy themselves with one another. They turn to one another and try to understand each other and then they discover that they have never understood one another. Each speaks a different language. So the struggle between the two types begins. They discover they are two wholly different people; the values of the one are the negation of the other's.[2] The

[1] *Das Unbewusste im normalen und kranken Seelenleben*, p. 84.
[2] Cf. the description of such a struggle in Paul Claudel's *Animus and Anima* (quoted by H. Brémond, *Mystik und Poesie*, pp. 129-130). Animus and anima are used here to signify the two basic types of Intro- and Extroversion in the conflict of head and heart, conscious and unconscious as well as in the conflict of two individuals.

same phenomenon often surprises people as they move into the afternoon of life. Their energies are no longer completely absorbed by the problems of daily life, they are free and unoccupied and feel dissatisfied with life. They feel they must look for a new purpose in life. What has happened? It is the problem of the 'general change of attitude'. It sometimes happens that before marriage a man can be explained in Freudian terms and afterwards in Adlerian, which has, incidentally, always been the way of common sense. Extroversion is liable to break down when circumstances change as they usually do with advancing years. The extroverted man now has to try and understand his introverted wife and vice versa. The ageing person now has time to occupy himself with his inner soul and is confronted with the task of developing hitherto neglected functions. 'The problem of types suggested by the conflict between Freud and Adler evidently leads us into a new problem, the problem of opposites. It is obvious that extro- and introversion are two opposite, natural psychological attitudes or tendencies which Goethe once called diastole and systole. They ought to bring about a rhythm of life in a harmonious sequence but it seems to require supreme mastery to attain this rhythm.'[1] This problem of the change of attitude exists not only for the individual but for whole peoples and groups of peoples as well. Our present Western civilization is dominated by the extrovert attitude. Western man is inwardly sick as is demonstrated by psychotherapeutic experience. The two world wars were an outbreak of the latent forces in humanity. They signified the breakdown of rationalism and the return to irrational values. The basic difference between intro- and extroversion is also evident in the antithesis

[1] *Das Unbewusste im normalen und kranken Seelenleben*, p. 86.

between the Roman and the Eastern churches. The guiding principles of the East are wisdom, contemplation, the spirit of brotherhood, spiritual intensity, unity; those of the West are faith, action, organization, individuality.

Life itself confronts us with the problem of changing our attitude. From inside the process is like this: 'When a man is confronted with a difficult task which he cannot master with the means at his disposal, there arises automatically a backward movement of the libido, a regression. The psychic energy is withdrawn from the present problem, is introverted and inspires in the unconscious a more or less primitive analogy of the conscious situation together with an earlier way of adaptation.'[1] In other words, there appears an inferior introversion. Undifferentiated and therefore undisciplined, it lives and dominates the ego, instead of the other way round. Psychic energy has followed its natural gradient. The problem of opposites is an energetic problem. Knowledge of the laws of energetics in the psychic system allows us to look into the deeper stratum of the soul. We need therefore to deal now with the energetics of the psyche.

[1] *Über die Energetik der Seele*, p. 94.

CHAPTER EIGHT

PSYCHIC ENERGY

W E have often had occasion to use the term 'psychic energy', when discussing forgetfulness and repression, dreams and fantasies, and, finally, the problem of opposites. Does it signify a vital energy, a psychic energy, that constitutes the life of the psyche? The question is open to the danger of hypostasis since it is concerned with the contents, the material and quality of psychic energy. The danger lies in regarding certain phenomena as ultimate essences and substances which should in fact be traced back to a number of different stages of development. But these occult qualities obstruct the path of research. Natural science in the Middle Ages always enquired about the 'What' of a phenomenon and hypostatized all kinds of natural energies. What is the force of gravity which pulls the body down to earth? It was only when Galileo asked about the 'How' of phenomena, ignored qualities and investigated quantitative relationships and conditions that gravity was understood. He understood quantity in the way that physics continues to do today in regard to all expressions of energy and power.

The energy of the psyche has to be conceived in just the same way. It expresses a quantitative relationship. The quality of the psyche is an unknown power, an X. 'The psychic material is not explained, but psychic processes are set into quantitative-dynamic relationship to one another.' It is therefore not admissible to hypostatize the concept of psychic energy and restrict it to sexuality as Freud did. For reasons of 'historical justice'

Jung uses the term Libido, borrowing it from Freud, since he was the first to examine psychic happenings in terms of energetics and dynamics. But 'in a general psychological theory it is impossible to use sexuality, that is, one specific instinct, as an explanatory concept, since psychical energy-transformation is not merely a matter of sexual dynamics. Sexual dynamics is only a special case in a general theory of the mind. When so regarded its existence is not denied, but merely given its proper place'.[1] Libido is therefore required just as much as ether in the theory of waves in physics. It is absolutely imperceptible, a pure hypothesis, an image or counter, no more tangible than the energy of the world of physical conceptions. The libido is therefore merely an abbreviated expression for the energetic approach, which very much restricts its use.

The concept of the libido is founded on experience. Psychic energy always appears in the form of motion or power in specific psychic phenomena such as instinct, wishing, wanting, emotion, attention, efficiency: in brief, the powers of the psyche. The applied concept of energy therefore immediately enters into the psychic energies, and this has an unpleasant result. The application of the pure concept of energy to the materials of experience leads to a concretization or objectivization of the concept which means that a certain vagueness steals into the exposition. 'We shall never succeed in working with pure concepts in concrete descriptions unless we are able to express the phenomena mathematically. But so long as that is not possible, the applied concept will always be automatically hypostatized in observation by the material of experience.'

---

[1] *Über die Energetik der Seele*, pp. 51ff (English: *On Psychical Energy*, pp. 31–32).

Admittedly it is not possible to find standards of measurement for psychic energy. That is owing to its very nature. It is therefore necessary to rest content with quantitative estimates. And one further limitation is inevitable. The psyche can only be considered a relatively self-contained energetic system. It is relatively self-contained because there is no possibility whatever of separating psychic from biological processes. Psychic energy as a specification is embraced by the further concept of a life-energy by which man is fulfilled. This makes it possible to do justice to the relations between body and soul. An interaction between them might well be possible. But nothing scientifically certain is known about that so that we have to limit ourselves to the relatively closed system of the soul. With these two limitations in mind, it is possible, however, to examine the applicability of the laws of energetics to the psychic system. These laws are:

1. The principle of equivalence.
2. The law of entropy.

How far the energetic view can be applied to empirical material can be tested by these two laws.

The principle of equivalence means that every energy that is used or disappears somewhere, turns up again elsewhere in the same quantity in the same or a different form of energy. This is of great heuristic value in the treatment of neuroses. When a symptom disappears, for example, that has engrossed the attention of consciousness for a long time, or when it merely diminishes, the energy that has been released will appear in another form and one may expect to see an equivalent value appear in the shape of a substitute formation. The discovery of the substitute is not difficult when the substitute formation is in consciousness. But it often happens that a quantity of libido completely disappears without the emergence of a substitute formation. It also happens that a considerable amount of libido disappears as though it had been swallowed up by the unconscious. 'In such a case it is well to hold strictly to the principle of equivalence, for a careful observation of the patient will soon reveal signs of unconscious activity, as for example in the increase of certain symptoms, or a new symptom, important dreams, or peculiar, fleeting phantasy-fragments and the like.'[1]

The law of entropy is the necessary complement to the principle of equivalence in that it explains the way in which energy is converted. It states that the conversion of energy is possible only on the basis of a difference of intensity, a difference of tension or a natural gradient, just as electricity needs a tension gradient in order to be converted into light, heat or work. Admittedly, psychic entropy cannot be observed absolutely since, as we have said earlier, only a relatively closed system is open to human experience. In this system energy runs up and down until it achieves a final balance. Thus everybody speaks of the 'storms of youth' which yield to the 'tranquillity of age'. We speak too of 'confirmed opinions' after 'battling with doubts', of a 'relief from inner tension'. The libido follows the natural gradient. Is it impossible to shift psychic energy freely and arbitrarily? Is it possible to divert it from the natural channel and lead it to unaccustomed activity? Yes, to a certain extent it is possible. The will can achieve a great deal, above all for a short time. On the other hand, everyone will discover that the actions of the will move within a course that is determined from within and without. When one

[1] *Über die Energetik der Seele*, pp. 34–35 (English: *On Psychical Energy*, p. 20).

departs from that line and tries to lead life into a different direction, contrary to the structural laws of the individual and 'practises' and forces oneself for many long years, the limits of the will become plain. 'The will is only the sum of energy at the disposal of the consciousness.'[1] This sum of energy is embedded in the total energic system of the psyche; the will can therefore only move and work within this framework. The rôle which the will plays in Jung's psychology has been summed up by one of his friends in a little experience which took place on a picnic they had together: they came to a mountain stream which was accidentally blocked by broken stones. Jung stopped the conversation and cleared away the stones so that the stream could flow freely again. This attitude of love and service towards nature is clearly visible in this theory of the will. Jung has also derived the dynamic laws of psychic energy from nature. He has reduced them to the concepts of progression and regression. Progression is the daily advance in the process of adaptation, the continuous satisfaction of the demands imposed by environmental conditions. What happens if there is a breakdown? For example, a person arrives at a situation which can be solved not by the rational intellect but only by sympathetic understanding. The thinking function fails and the onward march of the libido ceases: the obstacle causes a stoppage. During the progression the opposite pairs were united in the co-ordinated flow of the psychic process. But a stoppage in the flow leads to their falling apart, for the antithetical function is energized by the regression of the libido: this process is called Regression.

In the thinking type, for example, an inferior, because undifferentiated, emotional attitude comes to the top. The normally matter-of-fact person flares up full of

[1] *Psychologische Typen*, p. 691.

uncontrolled feelings if he is confronted with an illogical fact which can only be clarified by tactful, sympathetic understanding. Progression can also occur extrovertedly, if the environmental conditions exert a predominant influence on its progress, as well as introvertedly, that is, in subjection to the conditions of the ego. The regression activizes the unconscious antithetical functions, which are introverted or, in certain circumstances, extroverted. 'The one is a withdrawal from the outside world, the other is an escape into an extravagant external life.' By the energetic consideration of psychic phenomena we have arrived, spiral fashion, at the same point as before, when considering the problem of opposites. It now turns out to be a manifestation of entropy. Consciousness is forced to confront the hitherto unconscious functions which have now been activated. From this confrontation and assimilation the way is opened up for a new progression. In this way the obstacle and the breakdown, even in neurosis, opens up the possibility of achieving greater consciousness and becoming more of a personality.

The following observation reveals the whole magnitude of the problem of the psyche: The inferior attitudes have been unused and untrained. They are still in an embryonic, undeveloped, archaic form. The contents of dreams and fantasies show that they are associated with the other contents of the unconscious, the repressed and forgotten contents, and are therefore covered to some extent with the slime of the depths. What this consists of may be gathered from Freud's writings: infantile-sexual, immoral tendencies of an unaesthetic, irrational and imaginary nature. All this has led to the disparagement of the ground of the psyche. But a more penetrating search reveals the germs of new life among these unpleasant materials. It is as though one had to traverse the basic slime to reach solid ground. When the libido is liberated from the contents of the personal unconscious, by the 'psychic corrosive methods' of the Freudian and Adlerian methods, experience shows that it is not in our power to transfer the available energy to any object chosen on purely rational grounds. 'The energies can be applied arbitrarily at the most for a short time. But usually they fight against seizing for any length of time the possibilities that are held out to them. Psychic energy is a fastidious thing, that likes to have its own requirements fulfilled. However much energy is available, we cannot utilize it as long as we fail to establish an incline.'[1]

With young people it is usually sufficient to loosen some of the ties of restraint and falsity of attitude, the vital urge looks after the rest. 'The so-called normal person is probably able to sever the emotional fetters on one side or the other by an act of great willpower, or, what perhaps usually happens is that on the slippery path of instinct he slides unconsciously to the other side, without ever realizing the kind of conflict that has taken place behind a few headaches or other indisposition.'[2] With people who have already lived a major part of their lives, and who are no longer inspired by any great hopes for the future, and have only long since familiar duties and old age to look forward to, we are faced with a different task. But even in younger people a slight neurosis often conceals some spiritual trouble which is the result of a dissension in the greater depths of the psyche. Proceeding from physical symptoms, therefore, we encounter spiritual causes; but we also see that the latter have still deeper causes themselves. In such cases

[1] *Das Unbewusste im normalen und kranken Seelenleben*, p. 77.
[2] *Beziehungen zwischen dem Ich und dem Unbewussten*, pp. 14–15.

the regression is so persistent and strong that the doctor can only wait and see. Experience also shows that the energy is already striving towards an incline and has already found a tie. Usually this is the doctor himself. All the fantasies suddenly appear to be related to him, in dreams, he appears in an entirely new light. Anyone who has ever possessed a friend and adviser or a kind teacher and has suddenly received a suggestion in the course of conversation which has thrown a light on the one-sidedness of his outlook and drawn attention to deficiencies and errors, may well have stared at the speaker. One is aware that he has intervened in the life of one's psyche and one has a vague feeling of the revolutionary consequences which will result. How does the man know this about me, what kind of gifts has he? He appears great and mysterious, one does not know whether one should love or fear him. On calm consideration the experience proves to be a transfer of one's own psychic feelings to the friendly person, who smilingly declares that he has no mysterious powers. With this experience which everyone can have our understanding of the phenomenon of transference is increased.

A medical analysis naturally goes still deeper and brings about momentous changes in the attitude of the psyche. And the doctor appears even greater, and simultaneously as terrible as a demon and as intimate as a loved one. What are the contents which are suddenly revived without and against one's will? What is the meaning of the emergence of these images, which are so strong that they can be projected on to another person? Has the energy that disappeared in the regression moved into these images? The latter are, however, only the beginning of new manifestations from the depths. For very soon the patient sees qualities in the doctor which cannot possibly derive from the personal unconscious, but can only come from some deeper place. If the patient realizes that the mechanism of transference is a projection of his own psychic contents, it will begin to perform a somersault, and new images will emerge, mysteriously and not immediately intelligible: *symbols*.

What has happened? Jung has used a comparison to illustrate the process. The progession may be compared with a watercourse which flows from a mountain into a valley. An obstacle such as a river dam blocks up the course and transforms its kinetic energy into the potential energy of the situation. By being dammed up the water is forced to take another direction, if it has reached a height which allows it to overflow. It flows perhaps into a canal which conducts the vital energy produced by the gradient to a turbine installation where it is turned into electricity. The transformation is an image of the new progression produced by damming up and regression, the changed character of which consists in its reappearance in a new form, in this case that of electricity. Applying this to the reality of the psyche we get the following result: 'The psychological machine, which transforms energy, is the symbol.' These are the problems that Jung has dealt with in his book *The Transmutation of Symbols*. The energetic approach has proved worth while. The quantitative relationships in the life of the psyche open up possibilities of knowledge about psychic occurrences which a purely qualitative approach overlooks. In addition, by combining the libido with the symbol they take us one stratum further down into the structure of the psyche, into the collective unconscious.

CHAPTER NINE

THE COLLECTIVE UNCONSCIOUS

IT was the discovery of the collective unconscious that made Jung's name well known outside the narrow circle of specialists. If in his analysis of the personal unconscious it was possible to see merely a continuation of the Freudian school, it was his research into the deeper background of the soul that established his fame as a psychologist for whom Freud and Adler merely provided a few basic materials. The word collective is used as opposed to the word personal. The personal unconscious contains acquisitions of the individual's existence; they are the private possession of the individual. But underneath them there is a stratum of the psyche which the individual received as part of his inheritance as a member of the human race. It is common to all human beings, to all peoples, to the whole of humanity; it is 'collective'. The shaft in the soul thrusts down into the centre from which the threads can be pursued in all directions and from which light falls on the strata of the psyche which react on the centre. There we shall meet all the questions that the problem of the psyche contains. At the nodal point the line which leads down to the body crosses the invisible way that leads upwards to the supreme heights, into the being of the mind. To use an image, the being of the psyche is harnessed between the two poles and all research will necessarily have to oscillate between them. This must now be demonstrated from Jung's own researches.

Experience is the sole basis of our claim to speak of a

spiritual stratum of the collective unconscious. The psychotherapeutic process was followed out above from the simple analysis of the personal unconscious to the problem of types and opposites. The latter gave us an insight into the inner transformations which medical intervention causes. The further the law of compensation which relates consciousness to the unconscious draws its circles, the more peculiar do the contents invading consciousness become. The ties binding the patient to the analysis become more and more inexplicable on the basis of the contents of the personal unconscious. The fact that gratitude, sympathy and love are shown to the psychotherapist is not extraordinary. It is an aid to healing in so far as it represents a reliable bridge, on which the contents of the personal unconscious can be reduced to their constituents. 'In this condition of transference enhanced by well-being a reasonable motif can kindle so much enthusiasm that a vigorous decision of the will can risk even a painful sacrifice' and the person of the doctor can be dispensed with without difficulty. But when neither healing nor relief follows, but a standstill in the process occurs and empty repetitions in dreams, fantasies and symptoms, it is a sign that the regression is still continuing. Into what depths has the energy sunk and what is it giving life to? Jung describes the overcoming of the dead end as follows:

'I enquired cautiously in the consultation: Tell me, how do I appear to you when you are not with me? Am I still the same? She: When I am with you, you are quite pleasant, but when I am alone or have not seen you for some time, your image often changes in a remarkable way. Sometimes you appear quite idealized and then again quite differently. Here she hesitated, but I helped her to continue by saying: Yes, in what way?

She replied: Sometimes you seem quite dangerous and sinister, like an evil magician or a demon. I don't know why I should get such ideas since you are not really a bit like that.'[1] In another case the transitional state had already reached the limit where the standstill begins to become unpleasant. The question was what was to happen now? 'Since I never imagined that I was blessed with that "sound common sense" which always knows exactly what to do in every tangled situation, and since my patient knew as little as I, I suggested to her that we could at least keep an eye open for any movements coming from a sphere of the psyche uncontaminated by our superior wisdom and our conscious plannings. That meant first and foremost her dreams.'[2]

Usually the dreams referred to the person of the doctor. Unmistakably the figures appearing in the dream represented the dreamer herself and her doctor. But the latter hardly ever appeared in his natural form, but curiously deformed. Sometimes his appearance was supernaturally large, sometimes he seemed extremely old, sometimes like her father, but strangely mixed up with nature as the following dream shows: 'Her father (who in reality was of small stature) was standing with her on a hill that was covered with wheat-fields. She was quite tiny beside him and he seemed to her like a giant. He lifted her up from the ground and held her in his arms like a little child.' The patient herself had recognized the fantastic element in the transference. She realized that the doctor appeared to her a semi-divine father-lover and at least intellectually she was able to distinguish the actual reality of the doctor from this appearance. Nevertheless the dreams were repeated and

[1] *Das Unbewusste im normalen und kranken Seelenleben*, pp. 131ff.
[2] *The Relations between the Ego and the Unconscious*, p. 128 (translation from *Collected Works*, volume 7, Routledge).

succeeded in establishing their fantastic viewpoint against the view of common sense. 'I naturally asked myself what was the source of this obstinacy and what was its purpose? That it must have some purposive meaning I was convinced, for there is no truly living thing that does not have a final meaning, that can, in other words, be explained as a mere left over from antecedent facts. But the energy of the transference is so strong that it gives one the impression of a vital instinct. That being so, what is the purpose of such fantasies? A careful examination and analysis of the dreams revealed a very marked tendency—to endow the person of the doctor with superhuman attributes. He had to be gigantic, primordial, huger than the father, like the wind that sweeps over the earth—was he then to be made into a god? Or, I said to myself, was it rather the case that the unconscious was trying to create a god out of the person of the doctor, as it were to free a vision of god from the veils of the personal. Was the urge of the unconscious perhaps only apparently reaching out towards the person, but in a deeper sense towards a god? Could the longing for a god be a *passion* welling up from our darkest, instinctual nature, a passion unswayed by any outside influences, deeper and stronger perhaps than the love for a human person? Or was it perhaps the highest and truest meaning of that inappropriate love we call transference, a little bit of real *Gottesminne* that has been lost to consciousness ever since the fifteenth century? No one will doubt the reality of a passionate longing for a human person; but that a fragment of religious psychology, an historical anachronism, indeed something of a medieval curiosity should come to light as an immediate living reality in the middle of the consultation room and be expressed in the prosaic figure of the doctor, seems almost too fantastic to be taken seriously.' The hypothesis that the transference points beyond the doctor and that the unconscious tendencies have a meaning beyond the human person is conditioned entirely by its heuristic value. The supra-personal target is like a goal expressed symbolically in a form which can only be called a vision of God. But how could it be a vision of God when 'the dreams swelled the human person of the doctor to superhuman proportions, making him a gigantic, primordial father who is at the same time the wind and in whose protecting arms the dreamer rests like an infant'?

The patient had had a Christian education but had abandoned the traditional Christian dogma long ago. Therefore the vision of God which occurred in her dreams cannot be ascribed to any conscious conception of God. Her critical concept of God was confronted by the conception of God as a natural spirit, who, like the wind, is greater and stronger than man, like the intangible air. How do God and the wind come together? Jung draws illuminatingly on the results of ethnology. The Teutons thought of Wotan in the wind. *Theos to pneuma* means: God is wind, breath, spirit. In Hebrew and Arabic the same word means wind and spirit. These facts shed a profound light on the youth and childhood of the nations, on an age which seeks for God in the womb of Nature when man felt himself enclosed by the 'original forces of Nature',[1] when there was as it were a magic link between man and the world, a feeling of unity and perfect at-one-ness with the universe as a whole, with the 'boundless ocean of the universe, to which men of the early mythical ages confided themselves with a feeling compounded of pleasure and fear,

[1] Leopold Ziegler, *Überlieferung*, Leipzig, 1936, p. 77.

comfort and desolation'.[1] Levy-Brühl described early man's experience of the world as a 'participation mystique', a term which Jung himself is fond of using to describe the psychic condition of patients when they are caught up in projections.

The dreamer's conception of God corresponds to the consciousness of the men of that remote era. The archaic conception of God reappears in a twentieth-century person whose conscious idea of God is infinitely different. An infantile image of God in the shape of a childhood reminiscence would take a different form. God might be a kind old father on a golden throne in heaven. But the age-old giant of the wind is not like this at all; he derives from a primitive, archaic conception of God, a primeval image of God 'which grew in the unconscious of modern man and developed into a living influence, an influence that should give us to think from the point of view of the psychology of religion'.[2]

Admittedly, only those who have had a similar experience themselves and are therefore in a position to understand it sympathetically, can have any idea of this influence of an archaic conception. The influences and experiences are clearly differentiated. They take hold of a person from inside, at the point where he imagines he is 'at home' with himself. They induce a feeling of spiritual transformation and renewal. There is nothing 'personal' about this image of God. 'It is a wholly *collective* image the ethnic origin of which has long been known to us. Here is an historical image of world-wide distribution that has come into existence again through a natural psychic function. This is not so very surprising since my patient was born into the world with a human

[1] *loc. cit.*, p. 249.
[2] *Beziehungen zwischen dem Ich und dem Unbewussten*, p. 30.

brain which presumably still functions today much as it did of old.'[1] The fact that the cure coincides with the revival of an archaic image of God is in fact a very common occurrence and in no way a mere coincidence. Experience suggests that the distinguishing mark of such collective images is their 'cosmic' quality, the relation of dream and fantasy images to cosmic attributes, such as temporal and spatial infinity, enormous speed and dynamic expansion, 'astrological connections, tellurian, lunar and solar analogies, essential changes of physical proportions and so on. The clear use of mythological and religious motives in dreams also point to the activity of the collective unconscious. The collective element is very often manifested by peculiar symptoms, for example, dreams in which one appears to be flying through global space like a comet, or imagines one is the earth, or the sun or a star, or extraordinarily big or dwarfishly small, or that one is dead, or in unknown places, a stranger to oneself or insane, and so on. In the same way such feelings as disorientation, giddiness and the like occur.'[2] It is not merely the name or the figure that is significant; the collective situations in which the figures come to life are just as important. One comes to understand such situations and themes as 'the struggle with the dragon'; the sea voyage by night; the unattainable object of great price; death and resurrection; heroism; helpful animals; magicians, witches, transformation; woman, mother and child; father; monk and virgin; spirits, demons, gods and devils. All the things appear which the enlightened West imagines it has overcome and completely seen through. And they have an energetic valence

---

[1] *Relations between the Ego and the Unconscious*, p. 135 (*Collected Works*, Vol. 7, Routledge).

[2] *Beziehungen zwischen dem Ich und dem Unbewussten*, p. 69.

which breaks all opposition and takes possession of the
rest of the life of the psyche. The unconscious takes the
lead! The same figures, situations and events can be
found, however, in the myths and fairy stories of all
nations. Does this mean that the soul has tried to find a
way of escape? Are folk traditions as it were the exterior
to man's interior life? Are they perhaps the picture book
in which we can discern the events and evolutions of the
spiritual life over thousands of years, a representation of
the collective unconscious? In that case the psyche
will be the nodal point of all the modern fields of research which have hitherto stood alongside one another,
such as ethnology, theology, the history of art and so on:
'and the soul is the bubbling spring, the hidden treasure
and sealed up fountain which preserves the water of
life'.[1] Man and the human soul stand once again at the
centre of all research! 'Modern psychotherapeutic research has re-discovered this fact.' With the aid of all the
above-mentioned branches of research it collects a mass
of comparative material and 'it appears as though from
this preparatory work a comprehensive science of the
psyche is in process of formation, the extent of which we
are as yet totally unable to envisage'. The whole history
of civilization is seen as the history of the extension of
human consciousness.[2]

Jung investigates the twists and turns of the history of
the development of human consciousness in his book
The Transmutations of Symbols. In the first phase of
the human race, its childhood, the libido appears
entirely in the form of the food instinct which provides
for the building up of the body. With the development

[1] *Eranos Jahrbuch*, 1936, Introduction.
[2] The Eranos meetings in Ascona are devoted to the study of these
sources. Their reports have appeared regularly since 1933 in the *Eranos
Jahrbuch*.

of the body new fields of application gradually open up for the libido. Sexuality is a later field of application of outstanding functional significance. It first appears connected with the nutritive function as is shown by the influence of nutritive conditions on reproduction in the lower animals and plants. But in the form of sexuality the libido attains the shape 'the enormous importance of which' justifies the use of the term libido. As the reproduction instinct the libido has also passed through various changes. First it appears in the form of the 'fundamental sexual libido'. As an energy of growth it causes the individual to divide and sprout. It can be seen, as yet hidden, in animals in which the nutritive stage is separated from the sexual by a chrysalis stage. From this sexual activity the basic libido has split up into various parts whose functions are maintained by a specially differentiated libido. The process of development is shown in 'an increasing consumption of the basic libido, which only produced reproductive products'. Further spheres of application are 'enticement and brood-protection'.[1] Subsequently a 'complicated relation to reality, a function of reality of its own' developed again. According to Freudian theory, its motive power *is* sexual: Jung says that it *was* sexual to a high degree. 'The genetic point of view sees the emergence of the multiplicity of instincts from a relative unity, the basic libido; it sees partial amounts constantly splitting off from the basic libido.' It is easy to see what a sharp distinction Jung makes between himself and Freud, by opposing a genetic concept of the libido to Freud's purely sexual libido. Whether Jung hit on the right answers in all the details of this difficult problem will be shown as research progresses. Presumably other aspects

[1] *Wandlungen und Symbole der Libido*, pp. 129ff.

which he has not seen will help to complete his conception. But Jung's great success, which Leopold Ziegler
praises as one of his greatest, is the discovery that the
separation from the original libido, the shifting and
differentiation of the psychic energy only takes place in
conjunction with an image or symbol which expresses
the process analogically. 'The transformation of the
instinctive energy occurs through its transference to an
analogue of the object of the instinct, just as a power
station imitates the waterfall.'[1] The process of the transformation of the original libido by the symbol continues
to operate; we enter into possession of it in the symbols.
In this way Jung returns to the great context of psychotherapeutic work for in the practical work with his
patients the doctor continually comes across such symbol
formations. They are above all archaic and sexual fantasies. Considered in terms of energy 'the regression goes
back to the sexual stage and the pre-sexual'.[2] The pre-
existent pathways which man has received with his brain
are awakened to new life. To be able to understand his
patients it is therefore necessary for the doctor to study
the life of primitive peoples as expressed in the old rites
and myths. It is difficult to enter into sympathetic understanding of early man's experience of the world. Early
man had a pre-scientific type of mind. To understand
his outlook we should have to strip away all the categorical definitions which intellectualize our perceptions.
Early man's experience was a 'pure correspondence of
images' based on self-sufficient, saturated, direct observation expressed in myths. Anthropology has given us
information about the myths of Eastern peoples, for
example, the Astral myth: The sun-god aspires

[1] *On Psychical Energy* (English: p. 47).
[2] *Wandlungen und Symbole der Libido*, p. 393.

victoriously to the heights, falls and goes down again in night and darkness until his radiant resurrection in the morning. It is a constant struggle of the god with chaos. Is this simply a poetic rendering of the revolution of the sun? Jung's theory is that these myths are psychogenous. They are a visible manifestation of spiritual reality corresponding to the course of the stars. 'Every morning a god-hero is born from the sea and climbs on the sun chariot. In the West he is awaited by the Great Mother who swallows him up at night. He traverses the bottom of the midnight sea in a dragon's belly. After a terrible fight with the night serpent he is born again in the morning. This conglomerate of various myths doubtless contains the reflection of the physical process and so clearly that, as is well known, many scientists assume that primitive peoples invented such myths in order to explain the physical processes.'[1] According to Jung the images merely imitate the physical proceedings, but they are based on spiritual happenings. The mystery of the revolution of the sun is the mystery of the way of the soul. There are various versions: the struggle of the god with the demon; of the son with the mother in whose dark womb he has to spend the night; the picture which we all know from our childhood of the struggle of the sun-prince with the water-snake or nocturnal sea dragon. The meaning of the old image always remains exactly the same. *The Era of the Sun God* is how Frobenius entitles the book in which he establishes the existence of this 'whale-dragon-myth'[2] in every mythology in the world, including the story of Jonah in the Old Testament. What is the meaning of the myth; to what does it

[1] *Seelenprobleme der Gegenwart*, p. 167.
[2] Leo Frobenius, *Das Zeitalter des Sonnengottes*, Vol. 1, Berlin, 1904, Book 2, pp. 59–219, reports on the various kinds of the 'whale-dragon-myth' and its occurrence in all five continents.

give expression? Chinese mysticism supplies the key:
The resolution is the way the soul has to go, which is
called the way of truth, the royal way, and the way of
salvation in the Chinese Tao. The hero or the light-
bringing sun ascends from the dark womb of the earth,
from the gloomy deep—like the brightly conscious ego
rising from the passive unconscious. The ego reaches the
height of noonday by conscious striving. A strong tension
between the two poles, which are as opposite as light
and dark, fills the soul. But consciousness cannot live
from itself; it becomes empty; and thus the tension falls
in favour of night and the hero, that is consciousness, is
swallowed up by the invading unconscious, the mother-
powers. Will the sun-god be victorious again? The myth
recounts that in the inside of the dragon the hero cuts
out and devours its heart. He fortifies himself with the
dragon's most vital part. Then he cuts open the fish's
belly or is spat out. Renewed and strengthened with the
wisdom of the night he begins once more to tread the
way of light. In the same state of tension and dissension
as before? No—he has been changed; he has gained
strength and knowledge from the heart that he devoured.
A variation of the myth relates that there is such heat in
the whale's belly that 'the hero's hair is singed off him
and he is born again as an infant'.[1] Consciousness has also
been changed by plunging down into the unconscious.
The new polarity between consciousness and the unconscious has now been taken up into a unity which is
formed by the periodical fulfilment of the resolution as
an attitude that is capable of being experienced psychologically but cannot be expressed in words. That is the
way of the soul 'which imitates the rotation of the world
and leads the latter deliberately behind the polarities and

[1] *Erlösungsvorstellungen in der Alchemie*, p. 20.

also beyond them into the region where all dualisms are resolved, to what the Chinese call the yellow centre. . . . One is free to think of the polar region either psychologically as the antithesis of Yang and Yin, light and dark (in Chinese), or mythologically as the sexual dualism of the begetter and conceiver, or cosmologically as the division between Being and Life, or again, psychologically, as the incompatibility of the light and dark soul, or even physiologically as the conflict between the heavenly heart of the brow and the earthly heart of the breast. Anyone who traverses this way of light travels at all events away from the sphere of polarity'.[1] The mythos expresses the psychic practice of the damming up and flowing back of the libido: progression and regression, and also the maturing of the personality by the conquest of resistance in the psyche; this is just as much the development of the human soul, seen collectively, as it is the growth of the single personality, seen individually, just as phylogenesis is contained in ontogenesis.

It is the mechanism of projection which relates the picture book of human traditions to the inner happenings of the psyche. We have already met it in the analysis of the personal unconscious. A process or content which resides in the unconscious confronts us as a quality of the object, of our fellow men or environment. The influences of the unconscious content are foreign to the ego, they appear to come from outside, from the object: they are projected. Subject and object are embraced by a bond of mutual dependence and involuntary mutual influence. If we tried to forgo all the contents of consciousness: the control of Nature by technics; knowledge of the causes of disease, of the human body and the forces of Nature;

[1] Leopold Ziegler, *Überlieferung*, p. 256.

of all intellectual faculties; the conception of a supra-
mundane god—what kind of a world would we plunge
down into? A world in which man is imprisoned in the
all-embracing play of events, a powerless link in the
chain of causal relationships, a world in which the powers
of Nature are personified as spirits or demons of whose
despotic sway man is the helpless victim, and which are
the cause of disease. A world in which the forces of love,
hatred, fertility, war have a sacred, divine character.
The god of war inspires man with the feeling of hatred—
man himself is not guilty! 'Sexuality appears as a god of
fertility, as a cruelly voluptuous female demon, as the
devil himself with dionysian goat's feet and indecent
gestures or as a terrifying, ensnaring serpent.'[1] Man can
no longer differentiate himself from the forces of his
environment, he has become identical with and completely involved in Nature. This gives a rough idea of
the archaic identity of subject and object which is called
'participation mystique'. The psychic forces act unconsciously outside the psyche, bound up with and mingled
with the object: they are projected. They are not subject
to the rule of the ego complex which is still very small.
They are unconscious and autonomous. Their mysterious, autonomous influence is felt to be magical, as
though it derived from invisible spirits and demons.
Magic and witchcraft are typical of the primitive
mentality: a fact which can still be observed today. It is
only the difficulty of a situation which demands a new
kind of adaptation that makes the conscious possession
of the forces of the psyche a necessity. The absence of the
projected contents and the lack of differentiation between
the psyche and the object are felt to be disturbing and
obstructive, and man is forced to take back the projection

[1] *Seelenprobleme der Gegenwart*, p. 170.

and, for example, to ascribe a sudden change of mood to himself. The process of taking back psychic forces that have been projected is called Introjection. The conscious ego takes in new contents, increases its size and is able more and more to differentiate between itself and its environment. The magic rites and myths of the various nations correspond to the stage of psychological identity with the world. But the necessities of life made differentiation imperative, and this was made possible only by the withdrawal of the projections, which led to knowledge of human nature. The revolving orbits of the stars were now acknowledged as the real form of the world. Astronomy took the place of astrology: only the psychological names of the constellations remained. Man now felt that he was the discoverer of the starry world. For a long time he retained an intuitive knowledge of the interrelationships of the natural world. According to Jung, alchemy was a final echo of this knowledge. The key to an understanding of alchemy is the collation of its results with the mechanism of the projection of psychic contents. During his experiments the alchemist had certain psychic experiences which he attributed to the chemical process. He was unaware of the fact that these experiences had nothing to do with matter as we know it today, that they were in fact a projection. 'He experienced his projection as an attribute of matter, but what he actually experienced was his own unconscious. In this way he retraced the path of man's developing knowledge of nature. As everyone knows, science began with the stars, and mankind discovered in them the dominants of the unconscious, the so-called gods, as well as the curious psychological qualities of the zodiac; a complete doctrine of character, wholly projected. Astrology is a primeval experience, and so is alchemy. Such projections always repeat themselves when man tries to investigate an empty darkness and then unwittingly fills it with living form.'[1] The alchemists' writings show that during their work they had hallucinations or visionary perceptions which cannot have been anything but the projections of unconscious contents: 'I demand of thee, look with the eyes of the spirit at the shoot of the grain of wheat in respect to all its circumstances, that thou mayest bring the tree of the philosophers to grow. Out of other things thou wilt never make the one, unless first the one arises out of thyself. The work must be performed with the true imagination, and not with the fantastic.'[2] All these remarks suggest that 'the essential secret of the art is concealed in the human spirit; that, as we would put it today, it is in the unconscious'.[3] In alchemy we also find the myth of the sun hero and his nightly journey in a characteristic allegory: the father (i.e. the unconscious) devours the royal sun (the ego); or the sun is drowned in mercury or is swallowed by the lion. Our fairy tales also appear in an entirely new light. The hero has to pass through perils to attain happiness. He has to penetrate a dangerous zone (deep water, a cave, forest, island, fortress, etc.) to find the hidden treasure which is the pledge of happiness (a maiden, an elixir or a magic ring). Even today man is still afflicted by these fairy tale motifs in dreams. They force the conscious ego to plunge down into its own depths, into the sphere of dark unconscious feelings and premonitions. Every healthy human being is afraid of and resists too deep an immersion in his own depths. He fears it may

[1] *The Idea of Redemption in Alchemy*, p. 213 (trans. by S. Dell, in *The Integration of the Personality*, Kegan Paul, 1941).

[2] *loc. cit.*, pp. 215–216.

[3] *loc. cit.*, p. 216.

be like a journey to Hades. But in fact the psychic back ground, this dark, unknown place, exerts a fascinating attraction which threatens to become even more over-whelming the more one penetrates into it. The psychological danger that one is afraid of is the dissolution of the conscious personality into its functional components. This disintegration into functional and sometimes actual schizophrenia is what the alchemist terms dis-solution into atoms. In psychological terms, the con-sciousness which invades this unknown place in the psyche has been overcome by the archaic forces of the unconscious. In the fairy story the hero who is afraid or tempted to look round too carelessly and curiously becomes part of the solid rock in the underworld. On his way he meets many of his petrified forerunners.

We have reached the heart of Jung's evidence for his theory of the psychic background of the collective un-conscious. We shall now indicate four different trains of thought on which the discovery of the collective un-conscious is based.

1. A man in his thirties suffered a good deal from hallucinations. In his quiet hours he was allowed to walk around freely in the corridor. Jung once met him there, blinking out of the window at the sun and moving his head backwards and forwards in a curious fashion. He at once took the doctor by the arm and said he wanted to show him something: if he blinked and looked into the sun he would be able to see the sun's penis. Whenever he moved his head backwards and forwards, the sun's penis moved too and that was the origin of the wind. Jung noted this in 1906. During the year 1910 he was pursuing mythological studies. There chanced to fall into his hands an edition of the so-called Paris Magic Papyrus, which is thought to be a liturgy of the cult of

Mithras. It contains a series of directions, invocations and visions. One of these visions is as follows: 'In a similar way the pipes become visible, which are the origin of the serviceable wind. For you will see what looks like a tube hanging down from the orb of the sun, towards the Western regions, as though it were an endless East wind. But when the die is cast to the other wind that blows in the Eastern regions, the vision will turn that way too.' Obviously this is based on the idea that the windstream blows through pipes from the sun. The patient's vision in 1906 and the text that was first published in 1910 are, Jung argues, sufficiently distinct in time for even the possibility of cryptomnesia on the part of the patient or thought transference on the part of the doctor to be quite out of the question. The evident parallelism between the two visions is undeniable. But Jung is also able to refute the assertion that the similarity is purely accidental. If this were in fact the case it would be impossible to establish connections with analogous conceptions or an inner meaning in the vision. Jung is able, however, to point to quite similar representations in medieval paintings. 'I can therefore', Jung continues, 'not find anything accidental in these visions, but rather a revival of ideas that have been latent from time immemorial.'[1] The contention that the mental patient was not responsible for the contents of the unconscious and that to use his hallucinations as evidence for the existence of a collective unconscious is inadmissible, is demolished by the fact supplied by psychiatry itself—so averse to the theory of the unconscious—that the contents of the fantasies of mental patients are often astonishingly similar to the contents of mythology. The contents of the unconscious swallow up the ego-complex

[1] *Seelenprobleme der Gegenwart*, pp. 161ff.

in mentally diseased persons and dominate the whole person. This shows the power that resides in these subterranean forces, once they break through to the surface. The study of mental patients and neurotics is therefore likely to yield more information about the unconscious than the psychology of the normal human being. It is a common experience that the average person does not reveal the full clarity of psychological phenomena but tones them down in the interests of a quiet, middle way.

Jung concludes from this case and a number of others[1] that he is entitled to speak of a psychic stratum of the collective unconscious, the contents of which it is possible to study in national traditions.

2. The next argument for the existence of a collective unconscious is based on the results of the analysis of dreams.[2] A twenty-seven-year-old officer was suffering from violent attacks of pain in the region of the heart, and a choking sensation in the neck, as though a bullet had become stuck in it, and also from pricking sensations in his left heel. Organically nothing appeared to be wrong. Analysis revealed that, shortly before the beginning of the neurosis, a girl with whom he was in love had refused his proposal of marriage and become engaged to another man. His pride did not allow him, however, to endure his pain and disappointment as a purely spiritual form of distress. His uncontrolled emotions came to the surface and after a few tearful effusions the 'pain in the heart' and the feeling of choking in the neck which comes from swallowed tears, disappeared. His consciousness had simply withdrawn itself from the unpleasant contents, so that, left to themselves, they were only able to reach consciousness indirectly in

[1] Cf. *The Transmutation of Symbols* and other of Jung's books.
[2] *Seelenprobleme der Gegenwart*, pp. 154ff.

the form of a symptom. What had taken place was perfectly understandable and, if it had not been for his masculine pride, might just as well have taken place in consciousness. The third symptom, however, the pain in the heel, did not disappear. The hope that, with the rendering conscious of the psychic pain a normal condition of grief and healing would set in, was not fulfilled. But a dream made progress possible: the patient dreamt that he had been bitten in the heel by a serpent and immediately crippled. This dream made it possible to interpret the symbol of the heel. The heel ached because it had been stung by a serpent. This meant nothing to rational consciousness. It must have arisen from a deep layer of the psyche beyond the reach of reason. The dream about the serpent disclosed a piece of psychic activity which took place not in the dreamer's modern individuality nor in his consciousness but in a deeper stratum of the psyche; only its resultants projected up into a higher stratum containing repressed contents, which confront consciousness as unfamiliarly as a dream. Whereas an analytic technique usually has to be applied to understand a dream, in this case a knowledge of mythology was required to grasp the meaning of an episode that derived from deeper strata. The serpent motif frequently occurs in dreams, even among the inhabitants of large cities who rarely see snakes. Jung argues that it is probably the same old serpent that has always been Eve's particular friend: 'Thou wilt stamp on its head and it will bite thy heel.' In a much older Egyptian hymn which used to be read or sung aloud to anyone who had been stung by a snake we read: 'He was stung by the venerable worm.' A woman had put it on the path. The patient's conscious knowledge of the Bible was lamentably scanty, but he had probably heard of the serpent's bite at some time or other and then forgotten about it. 'But something in the depths of his unconscious had heard of it and not forgotten it but remembered it when the occasion arose, something in the unconscious which expresses itself mythologically because that mode of expression accords with its own nature.' What were the events and experiences that had found expression in the serpent's bite? The serpent always appears in connection with a woman; it corresponds in the psyche to that part of it in which love, sexuality and the tension between man and woman hold sway. In the deep strata of the unconscious his experiences with women and his attitude to all forms of love found expression in the serpent's bite, suggesting that he was making a false response to the claims that this aspect of life was making on him. The underlying cause of the disorder was the refusal which he had repressed instead of accepting sincerely and honestly. 'But analysis also revealed a further piece of previous history which had never been apparent to the patient before. He had been the darling of a rather hysterical mother. She had pitied, admired and spoilt him to excess, which was why he had always lagged behind in school: he was rather effeminate. Later on he had suddenly adopted a distinctively masculine outlook, made a fresh start and joined the army, where he concealed his inner softness under an outward show of smartness. His conscious way of life was now opposed to his own nature, since his proud masculinity prevented the softer, more emotional and affectionate side from expressing itself. But these contents had penetrated far into the sphere of drives and instincts, and now found expression in the symbols of mythology: the old familiar and widespread images of the serpent and its bite. Many similar dreams dreamt by other

people and their parallels in the myths of every nation
forced Jung to conclude that this psychic stratum is
common to all men. The similarity 'extends so far that
one finds the same myths and fairy-tale motifs in every
corner of the world: a negro in the Southern states of
South America dreams the motifs of Greek mythology
and a Swiss business apprentice repeats in his psychosis
the vision of an Egyptian gnostic'.[1] This is what justifies
us in speaking of a psychic stratum of the collective unconscious. Only experience can establish its existence:
there is no *a priori* evidence in this field. An accumulation
and collection of innumerable cases and facts from
medical practice and every sphere of culture has supplied
us with a wealth of comparative material and turned the
hypothesis of the collective unconscious into the reality
of a background of the psyche which is the common
property of the whole human race. Depth psychology
has noted with amazement the independent expression
of the unconscious. 'No one, however, who has not
experienced it for himself will be convinced that there
can exist outside consciousness any independent psychic
activity, which takes place not merely in myself but in all
human beings. But if one compares the psychology of
modern art[2] with the results of psychology and the
latter with the mythology and philosophy of other
nations, one finds incontrovertible evidence of the
existence of this collective unconscious factor.'[3] But since
we do not know what the psyche is and know no more
about the substance of the psyche than the physicist does
about the substance of the physical, the field is open to
every possible kind of interpretation. Jung is not at all
keen on the term 'collective unconscious' which he has

[1] *Psychologische Typen*, p. 699.
[2] For example, Picasso. Cf. *Wirklichkeit der Seele*, pp. 170–179.
[3] *loc. cit.*, pp. 52ff.

used to describe the background of psychic life. 'One can regard the unconscious as an expression of the instinct for life in general, and connect the life-creating and preserving force with Bergson's "élan vital" or even with the "durée creatrice". It might even be feasible to relate it to the Schopenhauerian Will. I know people who feel the strange power in their own souls as something divine, for the simple reason that they have come to an understanding of religious experience in this way.' Whatever one calls the background of the psyche, the fact is that consciousness is influenced by it to an extraordinary degree and the less one is aware of it, the greater is its influence.

3. The Oriental Books of Wisdom are a further link in the chain of evidence for the existence of the collective unconscious. Jung has written a psychological commentary on three of them: *The Secret of the Golden Flower*; the *Tibetan Book of the Dead* and *The Great Liberation: An Introduction to Zen-Buddhism*. The extroverted European finds Eastern wisdom very difficult to understand. A study of it will, however, reveal to what an extent the West has become enslaved to the Object and how little it knows of the inner world of the psyche. On this matter Jung has written: 'My experiences in my practice have been such as to reveal to me a quite new and unexpected approach to eastern wisdom. But it must be well understood that I did not have as a starting point a more or less adequate knowledge of Chinese philosophy. On the contrary, when I began my life work in the practice of psychology and psychotherapy I was completely ignorant of Chinese philosophy and it is only later that my professional experiences have shown me that in my technique I had been unconsciously led along that secret way which for centuries has been the

pre-occupation of the best minds of the East. This might have been taken for subjective imagination—one reason for my previous hesitancy in publishing anything on the subject—but Wilhelm, that expert authority on the soul of China (and translator of *The Secret of the Golden Flower*), has openly confirmed the coincidence for me. In so doing, he has given me the courage to write about a Chinese text which, though belonging in essence to the mysterious shadows of the eastern mind, yet at the same time, and this is important, shows striking parallels to the course of psychological development in my patients, none of whom is Chinese.'[1]

The psychotherapist is faced with the task of healing the schism in his patient's psyche and helping him to find a way to embrace and combine the opposites. Starting with the physical symptoms he penetrates into the personal and collective unconscious. The aim of the way of healing which is called individuation is to bring the contents of the unconscious into unity with consciousness. That is also the purpose of the Chinese writings. In the Chinese Book of Wisdom the way of reconciliation is called Tao. *The Secret of the Golden Flower* consists of a description of the experiences encountered on this way, the dangers, the stages, together with warnings to the followers of the way. The correct physical attitude and the alternation of meditation with contemplation are described in detail. They are intended to bring about a concentration on the inner processes of the 'heart'. In psychological terms this amounts to the artificial production of the damming up process with all the consequences of a regression of psychic energy. The follower of the way of wisdom hatches out the soul. The

[1] Introduction to *The Secret of the Golden Flower* (translation from Routledge edition, 1931; trans. by C. F. Baynes).

'incubation heat' in meditation corresponds to the fire in the mystic's vision, the heat in the belly of the whale and the glow in the alchemist's flask.

In practising meditation one allows the soul to speak as a product of nature. One concentrates one's whole attention on keeping back the purposeful aspirations of consciousness and allows oneself to be swayed by whatever comes. The layers of the unconscious are awakened and activated and invade consciousness. Figures of demons and gods appear. The instructions of the book on this point are that 'the figures formed by the spirit fire are only empty colours and forms.' *The Tibetan Book of the Dead* declares that these gods whose intentions may be favourable or unfavourable are illusions which must be overcome.[1] The first to appear is the god of death, representing the sum total of all terrors. He is followed by twenty-eight mighty and horrible goddesses and fifty-eight blood-drinking deities. This bewildering chaos with its frightening attributes affords a demonic sight. But here too it is possible to discern a certain order. Reason enough, therefore, not to let oneself be confused and to make the mistake of regarding the illusions as concrete. They are rather 'radiations' of one's own psychic capacity. When Europeans speak of such qualities as martial, jovial, saturnine, erotic, logical and lunatic the words still show that these attributes are derived from the old gods. Those who practise meditation still experience them as figures of the unconscious. 'Many of the earlier gods have developed into personified ideas and finally into abstract ideas, since animated unconscious contents always appear projected outwards and in the course of intellectual development they are gradually assimilated by consciousness and transformed

[1] *Das Tibetanische Totenbuch*, p. 31.

into conscious ideas, and in the process the latter forfeit their original autonomous and personal character.'[1] And thus those who engage in meditation are constantly taught not to regard these figures as truth and not to mistake their faint glimmer for the white light of divine truth. To do that would mean losing oneself in a multiplicity of autonomous and partial systems and chasing after projected and concretized figures. It is dangerously tempting to do so, however, for at times their influence and power of attraction seem overwhelming. They are a direct psychic force! It is possible to divine the power they are capable of by imagining the state of those who suffer from hallucinations or insanity. 'The things we (Europeans) have outworn are only the word-ghosts, not the psychic facts which were responsible for the birth of the gods. We are just as much possessed by our autonomous psychic contents as if they were gods. Today they are called phobias, compulsions, etc., or briefly symptoms. The gods have become diseases; not Zeus, but the solar plexus, now rules Olympus, and causes the oddities of the doctor's consultation room or disturbs the brains of the politician and journalist who then unwittingly release mental epidemics.'[2] The task of the follower of Eastern wisdom is to see through the images and yoke the psychic forces which are concealed therein to consciousness, leaving all illusions behind him. This means lifting the veil of Maja and looking into a consciousness devoid of all contents (because without figures), and removed from all the contents of the senses. Consciousness thereby escapes from all opposites. This is the goal held out by the Chinese Book of Wisdom. The Indian calls it nirvana, that is, free from opposites. We

[1] *The Secret of the Golden Flower* (English ed. : Routledge).
[2] *The Secret of the Golden Flower*, p. 111 (translation emended by S.G.).

psychologists would call it a psyche which has taken back all projections. How difficult that is to achieve will become even clearer when we discuss the analysis of the collective unconscious. It is an art and a way of wisdom, not the result of rational decisions, nor a mere trick or deception. The long preparation that it requires consists in paying all the debts one owes to life, in other words, living through all the spheres of the psyche. It is an ideal that is ultimately realized only in death. *The Tibetan Book of the Dead* gives instructions for informing the dying and the recently dead about their bliss by reading aloud the texts of the Book of the Dead. The Book describes the ideal state, seen from the world of time and space, as the 'centre of emptiness' because it is stripped of all sense perceptions. Seen from above, however, it is the supreme light of consciousness, the unity in which there are no opposites, the purest and most perfect Being—God! In the course of a search lasting thousands of years, the East attained knowledge of the inner world, coupled with a childlike ignorance of the external world.

'We on the other hand will investigate the psyche and its depths, supported by a tremendously extensive historical and scientific knowledge . . . we are already building up a psychology, a science, that is, which gives us a key to things to which the East found entrance only through abnormal psychic conditions.'[1]

The Eastern books of wisdom clearly disclose the psychic stratum of the collective unconscious, which Jung has encountered in his analysis of modern men and women. It would be possible to collect analogies and correspondences with the collective background of the psyche from every field of human culture. Jung has

[1] *The Secret of the Golden Flower* (English trans. by C. F. Baynes: Routledge, 1931, p. 120).

undertaken the examination of some poems by a young American woman who produced them under the impact of overwhelming psychic occurrences. He has shown their involvement in the whole of human history. He has described this enquiry in his book *The Transmutation of Symbols*. Tremendous knowledge is required to trace the whole evolution of the human spirit. Jung has explored the most subtle inter-connections which a study of philology reveals. In all these researches 'the psychological precipitate of all the ages is studied. This material is anything but lifeless: it is rather a vital substance which becomes alive and active again when we turn our attention to it. The whole tradition of the human race constitutes an enormous depository of this kind of symbolical material. It is our task to approach these archives from a new angle by basing our enquiries more and more on the human experiences that lies behind them. Our feeling is that all the sciences should be grouped around man as the centre, as around a laboratory, by utilizing and assimilating all their results from the point of view of human experience. This is the consummation of the work begun by alchemy.'[1]

The fourth proof for the existence of the collective unconscious follows from what takes place in the analysis of the background of the psyche.

[1] Introduction, *Eranos Yearbook*, 1936.

CHAPTER TEN

THE ANALYSIS OF THE
COLLECTIVE UNCONSCIOUS

THE phenomenon of transference gave us the first opportunity of referring to the spiritual stratum of the collective unconscious. An image, an archaic image of God that lives inside the patient is projected and transferred to the doctor. Everything depends on the analysis and realizing in time that the image is being projected. But if the image comes from one's own soul, must one attribute the image to oneself, be the image oneself and be responsible for it? This is the source of the greatest difficulty in dealing with patients. Jung thus describes the progress of an analysis: He had explained the mechanism of projection to the patient (female) and made her see the necessity of taking back inside herself the transferred contents. She resisted violently: 'What, am I to be a man, and more than that, a sinister, fascinating man, an evil magician or demon? Not on my life will I ever accept that: it is nonsense. I would sooner believe that you are all that.' Jung reflects further: 'She is right: it is preposterous to want to transfer such things over to her, for she can as little submit to be made into a demon as the doctor. Her eyes flash; an evil expression appears on her face, the gleam of an unknown hate never seen before; something snake-like seems to creep up in her. I am suddenly faced by the possibility of a fatal misunderstanding. What is it? Is it disappointed love? Does she feel offended—depreciated? There lurks in her glance something of the beast of prey, the demon,

something really demoniacal. Is she then really a demon?
Or am I myself the beast of prey, the demon, and is
there sitting before me a terrified victim, trying to
defend herself against my evil spells with the brute
strength of despair? All this must surely be nonsense—
fantastic delusion. What have I touched upon? What
new string is vibrating? Yet it is only a passing moment.
The expression on the patient's face becomes quiet
again, and, as though relieved, she says: "It is extraordinary; I've just had a feeling that you have touched
the point which I could never get over in relation to my
friend. It's a horrible feeling, something inhuman, evil,
cruel. I cannot describe how queer this feeling is. It
makes me hate and despise my friend when it comes,
although I struggle against it with all my might." [1]

This description may suggest the kind of forces at work
in the analysis of the collective unconscious. One feels
their approach like the onset of a sudden catastrophe.
Consciousness crouches for fear of being engulfed at any
moment by the billows of the encroaching tide. The
forces may also appear in the guise of persons. The
whole wealth of possibilities of the collective psyche
descends with fascinating effect on the conscious,
bewildering and dazzling it. If the analysis has advanced
an 'unleashing of the involuntary imagination would
follow which is apparently nothing but the specific
activity of the collective psyche'. Undreamt-of contents
invade the consciousness. The more the influence of the
collective unconscious grows, the more consciousness
loses its pre-eminence. Imperceptibly it begins to follow
where the collective unconscious leads. An unconscious
and impersonal process takes over and without noticing

---

[1] *Das Unbewusste im normalen und kranken Seelenleben*, pp. 132ff (English
trans. 1928, p. 96).

it the conscious personality is shifted about like a pawn on the chessboard of an unknown player. Who is this player who decides the outcome of the fateful game? The aim of the analytical method is to reveal this unknown third force, as we shall see.

Once the unconscious has been aroused it exerts a peculiar and irresistible attraction. It influences the whole conscious trend of life and upsets its whole balance. This disturbance is brought about artificially by analysis with the medical purpose of solving the difficulties which hamper development. The upsetting of the balance will certainly occur during analysis, if not before the treatment has started, and usually even without assistance from the doctor. 'It often seems as if these people had merely been waiting for a reliable person to surrender themselves to and for an opportunity to collapse.' Fundamentally, the loss of balance resembles a psychotic disturbance, 'it only differs from the opening phase of a mental illness in that in its later development it leads to greater health whereas the latter leads to greater destruction'. 'Panic has broken out in the soul; in utter hopelessness it lets everything go.' The desperate efforts to overcome this condition end in a disintegration of the will. The energy which is released disappears in the unconscious. In such moments, however, the first sign of unconscious activity appears. Forces suddenly appear in consciousness which exert a mysteriously dissolving influence on the conscious personality. A psychic inflation takes place. The personality oversteps its own frontiers and feels borne aloft, inflated; to an outsider it often seems as though the personality is puffed up. This kind of inflation can be observed even when the personal unconscious is being rendered conscious. Now, the supra-personal, collective contents are not simply dead or indifferent material; they are, on the contrary, living elements which exert an attraction on consciousness. Will the ego be drowned in the torrent? That would mean a dissolution of the personality equivalent to a mental disease. If the ego is too weak to withstand the assault of the collective contents—which is not yet the case if it feels overwhelmed and submerged by the waves of the unconscious like a boat, provided it works its way up to the surface again—if the ego lacks the strength it will be dissolved and the personality will be indistinguishably absorbed by the collective contents. Then the neurosis will have merged into a psychosis, or, to put it more accurately, the psychosis was already lurking behind the neurosis, since the weaknesses of personality in question are usually innate, with their roots in spiritual as well as physical conditions. This is the proper sphere of psychiatry.[1]

This may be a good place to refer to the dangers involved in the analysis of the collective unconscious and the responsibility that rests on the analyst. Just as 'big surgery' is only practised by specialists, so 'big analysis' is reserved for the expert, i.e. the medically trained psychotherapist. The country doctor is fully aware, however, of the potentialities of his great colleague, the surgeon, and, similarly, the teacher, the clergyman, and the working doctor should be aware of the methods of big analysis—in order to realize their own limitations. Similarly, if psychotherapists and clergy are to work together, it is absolutely essential that the latter should be acquainted with the psychotherapist's sphere of activity. There are various possible attitudes to the collective psyche. The analyst's task is to lead the patient to the one that is appropriate and to be helpful

[1] *loc. cit.*, p. 44.

in the encounter. The first possibility is the pathological overcoming of the contents from the depths which we just discussed. The second possibility is an uncritical belief in the archaic figures. Anyone who takes this line is guilty of a serious misunderstanding, in that he conceives concretely images which are the expression of spiritual energies. He experiences ghosts and ghostlike appearances as reality. He has relapsed into an earlier phase of humanity by identifying himself with the collective psyche. This leads to certain definite results. If he identifies himself with the unpleasant, dark, black, evil figures, the powers of the devil, man will suffer a feeling of inferiority and move about with a bad conscience like a pitiful handful of humanity. But if he experiences the good gifts and powers as his own, he feels he is a 'reformer, prophet and martyr' who is sacrificing life itself for his 'calling'. Sectarians, leaders and disciples alike, belong to this category. They are involved in a kind of pregnancy of their own importance which prevents all effective self-criticism. If, before, they were hidden in a modest existence, inflated by identification with the collective psyche they now suddenly rise to the surface. 'Weak minds which, as is so often the case, have at their disposal an all the greater measure of vanity, ambition and irrelevant naïvety run no small danger of succumbing to this temptation.' These people have been swallowed up by the powers of the underworld, they have stuck fast on the way to the 'magic ring', since they have yielded to temptation, from fear, curiosity or vanity—as the fairy tale says. And thus these puffed-up individuals live not in reality but in a phantom world since their personal psyche has become merged with the collective psyche. It is not possible to restore the distinction between the personal and collective psyche simply by rejecting the awakened contents of the unconscious as nonsense and contenting oneself with one's own small personal ego. Jung calls this wrong track 'regressive restoration'. Those who take it prove to themselves and their surroundings that they are essentially small-size personalities. For what we are confronted with here are not mere possibilities which it is open for everyone to choose as he likes but with hard necessities of life. The awakened collective psyche drives man into spiritual trouble. He has to deal with its contents. The fourth and right way to meet the collective psyche leads to a critical analysis, to discrimination and synthesis. This is the way of individuation.

'One will come nearest to the truth, if one supposes that our conscious and personal psyche is based on the broad foundation of an inherited and general mental disposition which as such is unconscious, and that the relation of our personal psyche to the collective psyche is roughly that of the individual to the community.'[1] The individual has social duties but he must not be absorbed by the mass: he must discriminate. The individual and society are divided from one another like two poles, between which life oscillates. In the psyche the corresponding qualities are individual and collective. Both must be kept apart, clearly distinguished from one another. Identification with and rejection of the collective psyche are both wrong. What is necessary is a higher consciousness. Where is the narrow path, the royal path, the path of salvation, the secret initiation, or whatever different peoples may call it? 'This is the way of individuation. Individuation means becoming an individual being, in so far as we understand by individuality our innermost, ultimate and incomparable uniqueness; it

[1] *loc. cit.*, p. 45.

means becoming one's own self. One might translate individuation as the realization of selfhood.'[1] The self to be striven for is not the same as the conscious psyche or the ego. The individual psyche is confronted by the collective psyche as its opposite pole. Life moves backwards and forwards between the two. The experience of those who expose themselves to this process is the feeling of something new arising in themselves. A higher unity begins to embrace both poles and its centre is the 'Self'. The ego, the centre of consciousness, is no longer the centre of the personality. The Self constitutes the new centre of the basic personality. The whole psyche is taken captive by an ineffable experience which to the conscious mind is no more than a presentiment and a feeling. Everything is centred on the new-found unity. This is at once a solution and a release. Analysis reveals the way that can lead to it.

There are many cases which can be settled by the dissolution of a transference and its reference back to the elements of the personal unconscious. But if the attempt to release the transference fails, the doctor must decide to bring about an encounter with the contents of the collective unconscious. Analysis then performs the function of releasing unconscious proceedings which invade consciousness in the form of fantasies, dreams, depressions and emotions. Solution, interpretation and purely intellectual understanding are useless here.

A patient is suffering from a psychogenic depression. He has the following vision: 'He sees his fiancée running down the street to the river. It is winter and the river is frozen. She runs out on the ice and he follows her. She goes a long way out and the ice breaks; a dark crevice appears and he is afraid she may fall in. In fact she does

[1] *loc. cit.*, p. 31.

fall into the crack in the ice and he watches her sadly'[1]—
instead of jumping in and helping her out. His imagination is as it were crippled. By whom? The patient is
suffering from all kinds of depressing ideas, such as that
he is unfit for anything and hopelessly incapacitated by
his heredity. Intellectually he realizes that these feelings
are wrong 'but nevertheless they persist. They cannot be
overcome intellectually, for they have no intellectual or
rational foundation but are based on an irrational, unconscious dream life beyond the reach of conscious
criticism.' In such cases the unconscious must be given
a chance to produce its fantasies and the above fragment
is the product of such unconscious activity of the
imagination. There is no point in further investigation
to bring the causes of the case to light. The psychic
energy is swallowed up by the unconscious; it can come
to light and be removed from the unconscious only by
the roundabout way of images and symbols. Therefore
the patient has to make the courageous decision to let the
depressing images rise up though he is so afraid of them.
At the same time he must go outside them in order to
observe them. 'When a fit of depression attacks him he
must not force himself to work in order to forget it but
he must accept his depression and to a certain extent
allow it free play.' The difficult task is to let oneself go
psychically, to 'cede the mechanism of self-expression to
the happenings in the unconscious' and to take the dream
seriously. It is wrong to condemn this as equivalent to
surrendering to a passing mood. What is required is not
weakness and spineless surrender but something that is
difficult to achieve. In spite of being led by one's mood
one has to remain objective and make the mood an
object instead of allowing it to become a dominating

[1] *loc. cit.*, pp. 162ff.

subject. The patient has to try to let his mood speak. The mood must speak and reveal itself and show how it can be expressed analogically. The depressive fantasies are therefore a 'visualized' mood.

If he had not succeeded in remaining objective towards his mood—and how difficult that is anyone can imagine who is able to feel his way into the structure of a fantasy—if he had not let the fantasy speak for itself, but suppressed it, or if he had become absorbed by the feeling of hopelessness instead of observing himself, then instead of the fantasy image he would have had merely the paralysing feeling of being incurable and doomed to destruction. But in this way it was possible for the mood to express itself in an image and the small amount of libido or unconscious creative activity contained in it was withdrawn from the unconscious and incorporated in consciousness, in the form of an image. Jung also gives his patients an opportunity to draw their fantasy impressions. The idea is that they should simply reproduce how and what they feel.[1]

How can the man be healed? His depression is a compensatory reaction to his one-sided, intellectual and rational approach. He clings to his intellectual world and fights against his neurosis with purely rational weapons. His conscious world is cold, empty and grey. In contrast to that world there flow from the unconscious rich fantasy images, but others too of dark gloomy values. Shall he make himself suddenly unintellectual now and obey his feelings? He does not possess them at all since they are in the unconscious and have developed into autonomous complexes as a result of continued neglect. The patient had not taken seriously a part of

[1] Cf. the illustrations in the *Eranos Yearbook* and in *The Secret of the Golden Flower*.

his soul, the irrational. It was merely an irksome obstacle in the struggle to attain his life's object; this was how he had assessed the expressions of his feelings. He had fought against Nature, lived unnaturally and departed from the reality of his actual created self. But the 'gods' did not grant him success; he fell a victim to their vengeance inasmuch as they obstructed his path in the form of autonomous complexes. The naïve conception of the jealousy and vengeance of the gods is identical with the psychological conception of the projection of autonomous contents. But now the patient must take his fantasies seriously and impute reality to the irrational. Intellectually that could be done quite quickly but the soul laughs at the 'deception'. Victory is achieved only in the open struggle of consciousness against the unconscious, i.e. in the hard reality of daily life and in an inner struggle with the uprising feelings and their concrete images. The internal driving force must be experienced, felt and known. This demands courage, for it is a leap into the gloom of the half-light. The venture and the risk are the proof that the fantasy is being taken seriously and the unconscious recognized as real. This will lead to a victory over the one-sidedly intellectual point of view and the irrational impulse of the unconscious will be able to enter into consciousness. What is required is a complete experience of the unconscious. Jung explains how difficult that is in reality: 'My real world is threatened by fantastic unreality. It is almost impossibly difficult to forget even for a moment that all this is only fantasy, a product of the imagination which appears to be absolutely arbitrary and artificial, how can one declare that such things are real, how can one take them seriously?'[1]

---

[1] *Beziehungen zwischen dem Ich und dem Unbewussten*, pp. 167ff.

The all-important thing is to understand what is meant by the concept of psychic reality. Man experiences psychic forces and impulses expressed in fantasy images. They have become absorbed in and completely fused with images and symbols. The patient must experience them, as they come, and with no secret enmity. 'So long as we are involved in the experience of the fantasies they cannot be taken literally enough.' This complete experience of the fantasies is of crucial importance and an intellectual understanding of them must be admitted only in so far as it is merely a part of the total experience. The understanding is part of the experience. 'The important thing is not the meaning and the understanding of the fantasies but the experience itself.' Try to imagine yourself in the suicide scene described above, or try to imagine being afraid of a monster rising up before you! Or try letting in a witch with a poisonous drink (note the emotional value). Or, to put it in more up-to-date terms, try racing to a precipice in a motor-car and experiencing the fear as you hover over the edge and roar down the side. Plunging into an abyss on a mountain tour, the deep fall is transformed into the well-shaft, which leads into the unpleasantly hot, stupefying centre of the motherly earth! And to say that that is real? Man has an uncanny tendency to affirm the expression and not to separate it from the active element in the images. 'All the dislike for fantasy and all the critical depreciation of the unconscious arises at the deepest level from fear of this tendency to concretize the fantasy.' This tendency to concretize must be overcome but this implies that as soon as the question of interpretation is tackled, the fantasies must not be taken literally. If the experience is to be understood as well as experienced, the appearance, that is the fantasy image, must no longer be identified with the active element behind it. The appearance is not the thing itself but merely its expression. It is the expression of something unknown, but real because it is active. Reality is that which acts. 'Even the shrewdest philosopher can be the absolute victim of a perfectly nonsensical agoraphobia. Our wonderful scientific reality does not shield us in the slightest from the so-called unreality of the unconscious. Something behind the veil of fantasy images acts.' The tragedy is that it is split off from consciousness. The sharp division between consciousness and the unconscious and their antithesis is always a sign of neurotic natures teeming with conflicts. The conscious approach is one-sided, it gives an absolute preference to one or two functions, and the others are thereby forced into the background. By making the fantasies conscious and experiencing them, the unconscious and inferior functions are assimilated into consciousness; naturally this process has a far-reaching effect on the whole attitude of consciousness. The active participation in the fantasy process has a threefold result, as Jung has seen in a 'very great number of cases'.[1]

1. Consciousness is extended, since innumerable contents become conscious.

2. The dominating influence of the unconscious is gradually reduced.

3. A change of personality takes place in the form of a general change of attitude. Jung calls this process, which we have already met in the analysis of the personal unconscious, the 'transcendent function'. The psychic complexes transcendent to consciousness are deprived of their autonomy and 'yoked on to' or assimilated by consciousness, thus becoming a function of the conscious personality. In this way the analytical method of

[1] *loc. cit.*, p. 171.

dissolution finally turns to synthesis and the building up of the personality.

The above fantasy fragment of the fiancée who drowns herself is therefore merely an appearance and an expression of a happening in the reality 'within'. And the fiancée is not to be sought for concretely 'outside', she is rather a figure for the something in the patient which commits suicide. If she were identical with his real 'objective' fiancée the interpretation of the fantasy would remain on the objective level and the analytically destructive method would have to be used which dissects the contents of the dream or fantasy into reminiscence complexes and looks for its connection with a real situation.[1] The analysis would then possibly establish an unconscious tendency for the fiancé to get away from the fiancée because he is not suitable for her. The patient is engaged and the relation to his fiancée is the only thing that keeps him in the world at all. If he wanted to leave her, as the interpretation of the fantasy fragment on the objective level would suggest that he does, his position would be hopeless, since then the only emotional tie binding him to the world would be broken. All this would not be so bad, however, if he were extroverted. Then he would be better able to establish a relationship again. But the patient is introverted. His relationships are therefore regulated by inner facts. He finds it difficult to establish relationships with people, so if he were to surrender this last tie he would only injure himself and the process would be senseless. The interpretation must take a 'Copernican turn'.

Now Jung turns to an interpretation on the subjective level. He does not analyse any further: that would be merely marking time. Analysis leads to mere repetition

[1] *Das Unbewusste im normalen und kranken Seelenleben*, p. 122.

and becomes monotonous. There is also nothing more
to be analysed but an element speaks from the inner self.
The fiancée of the fantasy fragment is therefore also a
symbol of a complex in his soul, which Jung calls the
Anima. The Anima embraces the whole fullness of
possible relationships to itself, to the surrounding world,
to man, in a word, everything which makes the heart
vibrate. It includes the capacity for the slightest, loving
attention and its consummation in the striving for inner
union in sex and Eros. But this was what the patient had
never lived: on the contrary, he had refused it all claim
to live and had repressed it. 'Therefore the fantasy also
expressed the fact that his Anima disappears again in the
unconscious without being hindered by him.' The mood
is stronger than he, for he watches passively, instead of
intervening and holding fast and saving the Anima (represented by the fiancée). The unconscious shows a
tendency to turn away from the world of consciousness.
The patient ought to take a more vigorous and active
part in the process by letting his moods and feelings
speak, by observation and sympathy and living through
them. By restoring a natural flow he will gradually withdraw energy from the unconscious and feed it to consciousness and bring the depression to an end. At this
point the interpretation on the subjective level becomes
clear. All the figures and images represent inner, subjective factors. Every fantasy fragment and everything in
the dream signifies something in the dreamer himself.
'The dream is that theatre where the dreamer is the
stage, the actor, the prompter, the producer, the author,
the public and the critic.'[1] The interpretation on the
subjective level is therefore a synthetic or constructive
process, which detaches the dream contents from the

[1] *Über die Energetik der Seele*, p. 162.

actual causes, interprets them as tendencies or interests of the subject and tries to attach them to the subject again. Interpretation on the subjective level must be used in the analysis of the collective unconscious.

Once the process of attachment and assimilation is finished, the personality should be in full possession of its potentialities and completely itself for the first time. And with this we meet the goal of individuation again from another angle. But to grasp the whole range and significance of this process of first becoming a personality, the contents of the collective unconscious must be examined more closely. What does Jung understand by the Anima? Are there still further complexes of that kind? Experience shows in the regular course of a depth analysis that behind the changing figures and forms of the symbols the same content is always hidden. Jung has called these dominants of the collective unconscious 'Archetypes'.

CHAPTER ELEVEN

THE ARCHETYPES

JUST as everything in the world is articulated and not an indistinguishable homogeneous mass, so the spiritual background of the collective unconscious is differentiated. Various details can be distinguished. They are in the nature of complexes and units, firmly established and tending in a certain direction. In analysis one comes upon these dominants with a regularity that indicates the existence of an underlying law. When they emerge in a pattern, in the disguise of a figure or symbol, they attempt to dominate the whole consciousness, which is why Jung first called them dominants of the collective unconscious. When he had acquired more knowledge of their nature, another quality was seen to be more comprehensive.

In accordance with their collective and universal nature they do not appear to be acquired but inherited. The fundamental facts of life are always inherited. Thus the human organism is organized *a priori* for a particular kind of world in which water, light, air, salt, carbohydrates and so on exist. In this physical structure man is prepared for that kind of world. But his psychic world is also related to the conditions of the outside world and therefore as a psychic being man must also be adapted to his environment. Man could have no experiences at all if he was not born with the subjective potentiality to experience parents, a wife, children, birth, death, community, a profession, God. Man is born with a virtual picture of the form of world into which he is born. The images which are 'aprioristic categories' are collective in nature. They are images of parents, wife and children in general and not merely individual predestinations. These images must also be thought of as without content and therefore unconscious. They only attain a content, influence and finally consciousness by encountering empirical facts which touch and awaken the unconscious preparation for them. They are in a certain sense the precipitates of all the experiences of all our ancestors, but not the experiences themselves.[1] The historical factor of the dominants which reach back to archaic times, their significance as basic facts of life, as the 'beginning'—all these factors led to the adoption of the term 'archetypes'. In simple language it means 'primordial images'.[2] But the concept 'archetype' already occurs in the neo-Platonic Corpus Hermeticum which dates from the third century B.C.: to archetypon eidos. Jung adopted the psychological connotation of the Platonic concept of the idea, disregarding the metaphysical reference. In his view the psychological phenomenon of the 'archetypon eidos' is the empirical basis of the Platonic doctrine of ideas. Accordingly, in Jung's thought, archetypes are archaic and primordial images which have been imprinted on the psyche from time immemorial.

At the climax of the analysis or, from the patient's point of view, in the deepest and most painful abyss, they appear almost without fail. A new kind of figure appears in a dream or fantasy, accompanied by an overwhelming feeling of life, and to the extent that the

---

[1] *Beziehungen zwischen dem Ich und dem Unbewussten*, pp. 120ff.

[2] Jung writes that the expression Archetype is 'commonly' derived from Augustine, since Augustine also calls the idea 'archetypon'. He does not refer to any specific writing of Augustine. *Zentralblatt f. Psychotherapie*, IX (1936), p. 264.

figure is effective, the patient is released for his proper work in life. He feels that there is a meaning in everything again; he dares to act and is no longer afraid of picking up the wrong end of the stick. He is sure of his instincts again. It is as though man had had to traverse the whole road of the human race back to its source— in order to find his bearings anew at the fork in the road; as though he had to ask all the people on the road —his ancestors—how they would have acted in his place, what they have discovered to be right and proved by experiences of a thousand kinds to be the way of wisdom itself. The experiences of the millennia have deposited themselves in the pathways of the brain and thereby made us potentially ready to act again in the same way. The archetypes are the 'psychic aspect of the structure of the brain'. They penetrate our consciousness, when a potential readiness to act is awakened into activity. The 'Engramme' of Sémon are a kindred concept: they are the qualities which have been imprinted on our spiritual inheritance. All the experiences of all the ages have been deposited in the archetypes. They are the condensation of all that recurs in history, typical forms of human outlook on life. They preserve the oldest feelings and thoughts of the human race. Archetypes are the formulation of the results of innumerable typical experiences of our ancestors; they are a cross section of millions of experiences.

When the archetypes are brought to light and translated into the language of consciousness we experience them as dominants, as the archaic figures, images and symbols which were the reason for tracking them down at all. The archetypal images, figures and symbols are always charged with dark, purposeful urges and instincts. The archetypes are the perceptions or self-representations of these urges and instincts in the consciousness.

They are the manifestations of the instincts, that is to say, creative impulses from the unconscious. It is true that Jung extends the concept of instinct to 'all the typical forms of action, and wherever it is a question of regularly recurring form of reaction, it is a question of instincts, no matter whether the motivation is conscious or not'.[1] The sum of the instincts and their correlates, the archetypes, fills the stratum of the collective unconscious. They are the background of the soul.

The life of the psyche during the history of the human race is therefore reflected like a drama in the archetypes, and now the circle closes again: 'All mythicized natural processes are symbolical expressions of the inner and unconscious drama of the soul, which human consciousness is able to grasp by the way of projection, that is, reflected in natural events. Unconscious man finds in all the processes of nature analogies to the drama that takes place in the acting and suffering subject.'[2] Myths are the language of the archetypes. Therefore myths illustrate the whole history of mankind. Whole nations are able to discover their own character traced out in them. As the precipitate of our ancestors' experiences they clearly reveal racial characteristics. This is obvious from a comparison of German and Oriental fairy tales: the same destinies but what characteristically different ways of fulfilment!

The collective unconscious does not only provide an insight into the history of the human soul. Even more valuable and important is the fact that it enables us to find our bearings in the present and points the way to the future. The archetypes are not in the least the product of invention and conscious thought. 'They have gradually grown like plants in the course of thousands of years, like

[1] *Energetik der Seele*, p. 195.
[2] *Über die Archetypen des kollektiven Unbewussten*, pp. 182ff.

natural revelations of the human soul, containing living trends.' Through countless generations typical ways of acting and reacting have evolved in a process of selection, all deviations to right and left being eliminated and only the straight path has been transmitted so that the disciples of the twentieth century might find and tread the path instinctively. In reply to the question as to what moved the human soul to make these particular choices and keep to one path in spite of all the alluring bypaths and what is the meaning of the archetypes, Jung says: The archetypes correspond to the truths of life. 'The unconscious has experienced the life of the individual, of families, tribes and nations innumerable times and possesses a most vital and inward feeling of the rhythm of growth, flowering and dying.'[1] We must follow them, 'they have become psychological truths of nature'. The voice of the blood speaks from them. The archetypes are the psychological expression of the truths of life; husband, wife, child, father and mother, betrothed, nation, priest, God. May one entrust oneself to them? Jung says: 'Life is in fact the teleological *par excellence*, it is purposefulness itself, and the living body is a system of purposes which are striving to be fulfilled.'[2] Since the archetypes and what they reflect, human dispositions, talents and abilities, are unconscious, they can be only too easily overlooked. The background of the soul is covered by a very rational conscious life, which is mostly a child of its own time, that is, of the twentieth century. This is why the curve of the conscious life often deviates from the natural life, the 'fertile soil' of the soul, seen collectively over several generations and also individually in the conduct of the individual person. A gulf arises

[1] *Wirklichkeit der Seele*, p. 19.
[2] *loc. cit.*, p. 214.

between the unconscious and consciousness. The 'ego hangs in the air' and solidifies and goes its own way, highly 'reasonable' ways, but unfortunately in so doing it only too often conflicts with the 'truths of the blood' which are imprinted on the collective unconscious. The natural laws of the psyche are infringed. The basic facts of life and the world are ignored and life is lived contrary to nature.

Jung looks for a new orientation and fresh guidance from the collective unconscious. Neurosis is the reaction of the psyche to an 'unnatural' life. Its roots are all the deeper, the more fundamental the truths which are denied. 'To deviate from the truths of the blood results in neurotic restlessness; restlessness produces meaninglessness and this is a disease of the spirit.' Whoever, for example, is unwittingly still conditioned by his mother and father when already grown up and has not detached himself from them, has not gained the consciousness and experience of personal responsibility, creative strength and freedom and is suffering from a Parent Complex. He has not acquired authority, responsibility and independence. He has not grown beyond the infant stage and inevitably fails to meet the demands of adult life. Anyone who does not dare to live as a member of his own sex, does not become a man or woman at all, is basically opposed to the truths of the blood, one might even say, to the truths of Creation. It is understandable that the reception of these complexes into consciousness concerns and absorbs all the strata of the soul, including the intellectual, the reason and feeling.

It is in the religious sphere that the most serious results of a false solution of the problem of adult life become apparent. There is a religious predisposition in man, it is an archetype of the soul. Jung owes his recognition of its existence to his realistic, scientific method which is what enables him to recognize the sexual, social and other predispositions. How can twentieth-century man solve this his most important problem? The answer that Jung gives from his own experience as a psychotherapist is clear enough: 'Among all my patients in the second half of life—that is to say, over thirty-five—there has not been one whose problem in the last resort was not that of finding a religious outlook on life. It is safe to say that every one of them fell ill because he had lost that which the living religions of every age have given to their followers, and none of them has been really healed who did not regain his religious outlook. This, of course, has nothing whatever to do with a particular creed or membership of a church.'[1] The problem of healing is therefore usually a religious problem. In view of these insights it is certainly no longer possible to regard Jung as a mere descendant of Freud and his teaching as merely an extension of psychoanalysis. Freud's psyche evaporated in a 'chemical process of sublimation'. But Jung can rightly call one of his books *The Reality of the Soul*.

Jung has discerned the spiritual cause that lies behind the physical symptoms, he sees the psychogenesis of physical disease. But he proceeded to take the further step into the depth of the soul and discovered the collective unconscious. In the contents of the collective unconscious he has found a focus for the basic facts of human, natural life and of the supreme problems of the spirit as well: of sex, community, God. What perspectives this opens up for a therapy of the soul and for the study of the cure of souls! 'The hour in which psychotherapy was born struck when the attempt was made to find the

---

[1] *Psychotherapists or the Clergy*, p. 264 (in *Modern Man in Search of a Soul*, Kegan Paul, 1936).

spiritual causes behind physical symptoms, that is, to discover their psychogenesis, but our task is now to take a final step and see the human being in his spiritual need, behind the psychogene and beyond all the emotional dynamics of the neurosis, in order to help him.'[1] The doctor's concern for the patient's health passes into a religious concern for his soul; the doctor becomes a minister of souls. To a large extent Jung assumes the tasks of the minister of religion; how he does this will be the theme of the chapter on 'Religious Experience', which might also be called 'The Archetype God'.

The experiences of the archetypes in the analysis of the collective unconscious bring the whole man into play, the whole personality of doctor and patient alike. For both of them the cure is also an ethical problem. The most commonplace physical symptoms are often an occasion for studying the higher intellectual and spiritual problems of the patient. Is the dark but striving process within the soul to be trusted? Then dreams and fantasies must be considered the supreme expression of the collective unconscious. They are a message from the unconscious to consciousness and an attempt to point to the right way, in the symbolic language of the archetypes. The bride in the fragment of a fantasy described above was an archetypal image of the feminine in the patient's soul, an image of love in all its forms and relationships; Jung calls this complex the 'Anima'. This sphere had been wrongly lived by the patient; the way he had lived was contrary to the truths of the blood. But in the unconscious the readiness to experience all these truths was compressed and activated into an autonomous complex. All the psychic energy was collected there and all

[1] Viktor Frankl, *Die geistige Situation der Psychotherapie, Zentralblatt für Psychotherapie*, X (1937), p. 45. Cf., also by the same author, *Ärztliche Seelsorge*, Vienna, 1946.

warmth, goodness and joy was withdrawn from consciousness until it seemed grey and empty. The doctor persuaded him to listen to the language of the depression. But he was not yet able to and there was nothing left for the irrational contents but to disappear again into the depth, a proceeding which is presented in a dramatic form in the fragment of the fantasy. But once the patient is really frightened and shocked by an 'imaginative product' of the fantasy which seems unreal in comparison with external reality, and if he then has the courage to resist and to hold out calmly, then he will have taken the turn towards a re-adaptation to the bases of life which he has resisted in his soul. The way becomes free for the autonomous operations of the complex, and its personification in the dream will gradually assume a different form in future, if it should still be needed at all. The complex loses its energy and surrenders it to consciousness. The theory of neuroses, analysis and therapy have their ultimate foundation in the archetypes. Neurosis is a contradiction and antithesis of the archetypes; analysis must help to activate them; therapy leads to a reconciliation with them. The reform of the conscious attitude takes place in the direction of and in constant touch with the expression of the archetype.

Now it is no use delivering an erudite lecture to the patient on fantasy or dreams unless his feelings and perceptions keep pace with his mind. 'The patient can only accept what moves his heart as well as touches his mind.' It is not a question of learning a new truth intellectually —he has been living too rationally anyway—the patient must rather 'develop towards this truth, and in this way his heart will be reached, which strikes deeper and acts more intensely'.[1] Here again, in this coming to terms

[1] *Wirklichkeit der Seele*, p. 80.

with the archetypes, the doctor's therapeutic activity is merely an accompaniment of Nature and its gradual evolution. Admittedly he will need to know more than the mere concepts and tries to obtain direct experience of the contents of the concepts, for example, of the archetype Anima. The contents of the concepts can never be experienced merely by simulating the feeling of others. It is quite useless for an analyst to learn a list of archetypes by heart. 'Archetypes are complexes of experience, which enter, as though by fate, and their influence begins in our personal life.'[1] Only the person who has had the same experience will be able to understand the patient and the fact that he has shared the experience will be felt as a help in itself. Thus theory must always remain in the closest possible touch with full-blooded reality.

The best thing the analytical process can give to a man is his own discovery of his nature and the elements of his nature. The vital truths of life which he has found will become immediately clear and give the personality a centre of gravity. The helper must not upset the slow maturing of the patient by passing a hasty judgement. The helper must merely act as a careful companion of the spiritual process in which the unconscious has the lead.

It should be noted that the unconscious will retain the upper hand only if consciousness has gone its own way too long, away from and contrary to the laws of the inner world. The unconscious appears as a corrective and attempts to bend the path of life back into the right direction. Man then has to undergo the fateful experience of being conscious of the dark part of the soul. This is the positive quality in neurosis, that it can lead man to knowledge of his nature. Both halves of the soul, the light of consciousness and the darkness of the unconscious,

[1] *Über die Archetypen des kollektiven Unbewussten*, p. 212.

belong together and need each other; they are a 'self-regulating system'. They act like two poles between which life oscillates to and fro. The concept Soul embraces them both. The pure psychology of consciousness is as unfruitful as a single pole of an accumulator. Work, light and warmth are produced only by the tension in which both poles are fused. The concept of the Psyche also extends to the depth. One stratum rests on another. Jung compares the soul to a building of which the upper stories derive from the nineteenth and twentieth centuries. That is consciousness. The ground floor comes from the sixteenth century: it is a tower of the eleventh century which has been restored. In the cellar there can still be found the foundations of Roman walls, including caves that have been sealed up and on the bottom of which there are stone implements and the remains of fauna. That is a picture of man's spiritual structure today. We live in the uppermost story and are only dimly aware of the fact that the lower stories and foundations are so ancient.[1]

H. Schultz-Henke, an adherent of the Freudian school, has discussed the archetypes. His exposition is useful since it illuminates the subject from a fresh angle.[2] Man lives within patterns which are conditioned by basic facts. It should be possible to draw up a whole list of typical facts, such as the relationships between father and son, son and father, mother and daughter, and daughter and mother; between brother and sister; husband and mother-in-law, wife and mother-in-law and so on. The important thing is that there is only a limited number of basic facts which are determined by the existing order of things. Within this broad network of relationships we experience certain human phenomena so regularly that

[1] *Seelenprobleme der Gegenwart*, p. 179.
[2] H. Schultz-Henke, *Über die Archetypen, Zentralblatt für Psychotherapie*, IX (1936), pp. 335–343.

they become types of the human order: the peasant, the craftsman, the saint, the visionary, the ecstatic; the warrior, hero, priest; the Don Juan, the prostitute, the simpleton, the satanic man, the radical critic, the contemplative and the activist. 'It is perhaps surprising at first but if one surveys an adequate variety of ethnological facts, one begins to see that these types occur throughout the human world.' They are joined by a third group of a purely psychological kind: the ironical man, the sarcastic, the humorous, the irascible, the miserly and so on. No claim is made that the list is complete but, on the other hand, there is also some blurring of the frontiers between the various types and relationships. There are typical relationships between all these elements: initial relationships; later developments; typical endings: in other words, there are typical destinies. All this is seen from the point of view of man or woman and each sex sees it differently. Man has always tried to see the true pattern and to find a way in which the opposites are cancelled out as far as possible and the conflicts resolved. Therefore the inner desire for development in each type had to be cultivated. In the course of centuries or even millennia a great many irresponsible fantasies have been indulged in on this subject. But the bad, sterile, dead and inadequate fantasies have gradually fallen through the 'sieve of the collective judgement' so that only those patterns have survived which represented an optimum of order in the form of prohibitions and regulations, rites and acts of worship. The patterns which arose in this way were very largely irrational. Thought only helped to shape them in a purely clarifying and illuminating capacity. Emotional vision, emotional valuations and judgements were decisive. The fantasies about these patterns and also about unsuccessful attempts to establish them were deposited in the world of myth which is a condensation of them. Myths are the outcome of strivings which come from the depths of the mind and soul. Archetypes are the name given on the one hand to those primordial types which were enumerated above in various groups, and on the other hand, to those primordial images in the fantasy structures of the myths which reflect the patterns of the human world. They are therefore both creatures of fantasy and a natural reality. As creations of fantasy these primordial images develop an extraordinarily far-reaching influence. They are directly related to the deepest ground of human striving. They are Being and Vision at one and the same time. They are experienced as part of the substance of one's own person, and they meet all of us in the course of our lives; we imagine them to be an active force in the world. Their influence is felt as concretely as any natural reality. Everyone sees himself as a member of the first group and thus experiences an individual intimation and variant of the universal and typical. 'It is true that one can think about these types but they are not pre-eminently the object of thought—in earlier times people spoke of having a presentiment of them.' Taking Freudian theory as his starting-point H. Schultz-Henke does not conclude that all men inherit a common spiritual background, but he merely speaks of a 'tendency in man to experience the primordial images and of the relationships to them', which can be expressed in dreams and hallucinations. That is the reason for the striking similarity between dream contents, hallucinations and the content of myths. But their presence in the individual person is explained by the repression of uncompleted experiences of typical facts of life above all in childhood, and is thus restricted to what Jung calls the personal unconscious. The writer recognizes the existence and activity of the archetypes, although he interprets them in the light of the 'dogma' of the Freudian school.

But is the soul of the newborn child a *tabula rasa*—is there nothing at all in it? Or is the 'tendency in man to experience the primordial images and their relationships', this 'deepest ground of human striving'—not rather given to every child as a dowry when it comes into the world? Every child, Jung argues, comes into the world with a differentiated brain, predetermined by heredity and therefore individualized. And so it meets sense stimuli from outside not with a merely general preparedness. This in itself produces an individual choice and structure of apperception. These predispositions are 'demonstrably inherited instincts and even preformations conditioned by the family. They are archetypes.'[1] They guide every activity of the fantasy into its predetermined path and in this way they produce mythological parallels in the patterns of childish dreams and in the delusions of schizophrenia. To a lesser extent they can even be discerned in the dreams of normal and neurotic people. The totality of their contents corresponds exactly to what was meant before by the 'deepest ground of striving' and the tendency to experience the primordial images. In Jung's language it is the stratum of the collective unconscious, 'the expression of the various activities of life in images'.

The archetypes express their activity with the force and energy of a passion. The reality of the inner world is in no way inferior to the reality of the external world. 'Outside there is the rational world of the Here and Now, of the particular and the unique', of concrete men and

[1] *Über die Archetypen des kollektiven Unbewussten*, p. 268.

things, and definite concepts and values. Inside there is
the irrational reality of the timeless, indefinite, universally human, of ambiguously iridescent figures, fore-
boding ideas and indescribable feelings and constantly
changing possibilities.[1] Both realities are equally true
and equally determining. They relentlessly demand that
man should adapt himself to them. And yet both realities
are also incomparable and irreconcilable on the same
level. They belong to different degrees of the human
order. Thus the problem of their combination inevitably
arises again. 'It is the concern, perhaps the most important concern, of the single person to find the prac-
ticable "middle way" which unites the opposites of
external and internal reality, to mould his individuality
deliberately and in actual life and to do equal justice to
the world and the soul.'[2] Everyone probably goes a step
further on this path and comes to terms, unwittingly,
with the inner reality of the soul. At the end of the path
there is the new centre of the personality, the goal of
individuation. The treatment of this topic in the next
chapter will also shed more light on some of the archetypes.

[1] Toni Wolff, *Einführung in die Grundlagen der komplexen Psychologie*, in
Jung-Festschrift, p. 94.
[2] *loc. cit.*, p. 97.

CHAPTER TWELVE

INDIVIDUATION

INDIVIDUATION is a spiritual process by which the personality is built up. It takes as many forms as there are individuals. Only a very few people are capable of putting themselves in the spiritual situation of another. 'I cannot therefore'—Jung writes—'bring forward anything convincing, anything, that is, that will convince the reader in the way it convinces the person for whom it is the most personal experience imaginable. We just have to believe him by analogy with what we have experienced ourselves. Finally, when all else fails we can undoubtedly perceive the final result, namely the change in the personality.'[1] 'By analogy' with what everyone can experience for himself the attempt will now be made to describe the 'way of the centre'. It is the way that is taken out of sheer spiritual necessity either in analysis, occasioned by a neurosis, or owing to a situation in daily life that so shakes up a man that he is forced to withdraw to the centre of his being. Another way to individuation is through the inner urge to find and obtain the truth. But the 'gods' may bar the way and the person concerned falls victim to the vengeance of the subterranean powers. The inflation caused by the activizing of the collective unconscious leads to disaster: he cannot get rid of the spirits he called up! The 'philosopher's stone' only reveals itself when the innermost core of the personality is behind the search for wisdom.

Individuation leads step by step and deeper and deeper

[1] *Beziehungen zwischen dem Ich und dem Unbewussten*, pp. 174ff.

into the core of the personality. It begins with personal
appearance. Self-observation shows that we have accustomed ourselves to an automatic mode of reaction to the
surrounding world. It is a kind of 'mask', for its purpose
is to hide the individual's true nature and at the same
time to make a particular impression on the surrounding
world. Jung calls this arbitrary outer covering the
Persona. He compares it with the mask which actors
wore in ancient times, through which their voices
sounded. There is no connection at all between the
philosophical concept of the person and the 'Persona' as
conceived by Jung. For him the 'Persona' is a 'complicated system of relationships between the consciousness
of the individual and society'. Everyone knows the
official who has become identical with the part he plays;
or the always friendly, smoothly polite lady of gentle
birth. It does not escape the critical eye that the excellent
mask is compensated by a secretive private life. Anyone
who builds up too good a Persona for himself, reaps the
reward of irritable moods. There are people who imagine
they are what they represent. But the unconscious cannot
tolerate such a shift of emphasis under any circumstances as is shown by the following case which Jung
describes with the utmost clarity and frankness: 'I once
made the acquaintance of a venerable man—one could
easily call him a saint—for three days I went all round
him and could find no mortal weaknesses in him. My
feeling of inferiority became a menace and I was
seriously beginning to think how I could improve my
character. But on the fourth day his wife consulted me.
. . . Since then nothing similar has ever happened to me
again.'[1]

Anyone who identifies himself with a splendid Persona,

[1] *loc. cit.*, p. 127.

indeed, anyone who even attempts to do so, always causes unconscious reactions, moods, passions, fears, hallucinations, weaknesses and vices. In private life the 'socially strong man' is often a child in respect to his own emotional states, his 'public discipline' has a pitiable air in private. At home, his professional cheerfulness wears a melancholy face. His spotless 'public morality' is by no means so evident behind the mask. It is not even necessary to study his actions, his fantasies are enough. The more an effective and powerful rôle is played in the outside world, the more an 'effeminate weakness' towards all the influences of the unconscious develops within. In private life, moods, whims, and 'nerves', uneasiness and often a flabby sexuality, culminating in impotence, gain the upper hand. All this is concealed from the eyes of others and from his own eyes by the Persona. One of the first necessities on the road to personality is to part from the Persona, to detach oneself from it as clearly as possible, to strive to achieve a harmony of the inner and outer life and to be to the outside world what one is within. Sometimes analysis must take over the task but it can be solved without its assistance.

There follows a second step in the process of individuation. The contents of the personal unconscious are mixed up with the Persona. When they are analysed we see an image in a mirror which is calculated to reduce the overweaning ambitions of the 'spotless' ego. Everything that has been repressed, everything that is morally disreputable and unpleasant has accumulated there and now comes alive. It is the shadow of the brightly lit personality. It must be taken into account and then the ego will not undertake any pious and ascetic flights of Icarus and will maintain its measure and centre. Once our suspicions have been roused against the good side, there will always

be a vague awareness of the lower side and this will give a
feeling of balance, calm and security. For only the
unknown is dangerous. The shadow is the dark and
painful gate that must be passed on the way to the
collective unconscious. Once it is taken into account an
objective attitude to one's own personality becomes
possible. In dreams and fantasies the shadow appears as
a dark figure, as the powerful and harmful guardian of
the threshold. What is the result of being conscious of it?
'The more one becomes aware of oneself through self-
knowledge and corresponding actions, the more the
stratum of the personal unconscious with which the
collective unconscious is overlaid will disappear. This
gives rise to a consciousness that is no longer enmeshed
in the petty personal world of the ego, but shares in a
wider world, in the Object.'[1] Individuation does not lead
to individualism but it breaks down the barriers and
walls which the ego has erected between itself and the
surrounding world. The repressions, as understood by
Freud and the 'guiding lines' of Adler's theory, must be
resolved or exposed in this context. 'Becoming essential'
—meaning to advance to the Self—and 'becoming
objective' are correlative. To be objective means knowing the real object and acting with it, not with some
illusory object that is 'desired'. The process of differentiation from the Persona and the removal of the personal
unconscious which occur in the course of individuation
make one sensitive. It is as though a protective skin had
been removed and the naked soul exposed to reality and
its own experience. Consciousness comes into contact
with the collective unconscious and the uppermost layer
of the collective unconscious is a kind of counterpart to
consciousness. It is as it were its complement and related

[1] *loc. cit.*, p. 99.

to it as a man is related to his wife. If the consciousness of the male tends towards the masculine ideal, the complement represents the feminine in the masculine soul: the Anima. Jung's concept of the Anima has nothing in common with the Christian concept of the 'soul'. He means a part of the soul, an archetype which, like a magnetic field, attracts and holds fast everything pertaining to itself so that as a complex it passes from one colour to another. Every human being is physically and spiritually bi-sexual; the predominant factor determines the sex. If the consciousness is male, the female will be in the unconscious and vice versa. The feminine in the male is at the same time a preparation for the experience of woman as mother, fiancée and wife. It contains the natural relationship of man and wife. Psychologically the Anima is the capacity for every sort of affectionate and loving relationship. As the dark, emotional, pregnant and creative principle, the Anima is also the relation to the inner world, just as the Persona is to the outer world. This means that anyone who wishes to reach the further contents of the collective unconscious must first traverse the sphere of the Anima. The diagram overleaf (*q.v.*) may explain better what is meant.

The circle encloses the whole sphere of the Psyche. The smaller upper part represents consciousness with the ego at the centre. The Persona establishes relationships with the outer objects. The next layer under consciousness is the personal unconscious. The dissolution of the Persona and of the personal unconscious which proceed hand in hand leads to the meeting of consciousness with the Anima function which enwraps the collective unconscious. If the further contents are ever to be reached it is absolutely necessary to come to terms with this covering of the ground of the soul. (The arrows and the centre of

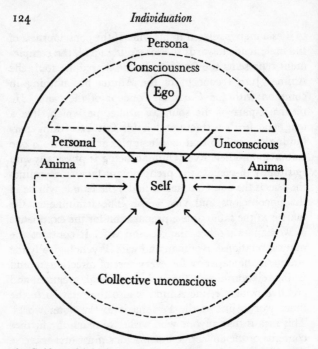

the Self to which they point, will be explained below: the
diagram can only help our conceptual understanding. It
comes nowhere near the spiritual reality of the mutually
penetrating energies and dispositions.[1]) The sphere of the
Anima (the Animus in woman) is so important that
practising therapists have been struck by the following
fact: the more the doctor has balanced the male-female
antithesis within himself and anchored it to the centre of
his personality, that is to say, has by individuation made
the archetype Anima part of his consciousness, the more
he can help the patient since he is not suffering from an

[1] Cf. the similar description in Joan Corrie, *Jungs Psychologie im Abriss*,
Zürich, 1929, p. 23.

unconscious transference, a so-called counter-trans-
ference to the patient, but retains his complete objectivity.[1] Probably the same discovery can be made in all
educational activity. If one ventures to speak of spiritual
harmony and perfect spiritual balance at all, the archetype Anima is the key to it. It mediates all relationships
with the depths of the soul.

We shall now try to show the full significance of the
archetype Anima. How do we get to know it? It is
already at work in the child, since it is the Anima which
bestows a 'superhuman radiance' on the image of the
mother. When this transference is gradually removed by
the triteness of everyday life, the archetype slips back
into the unconscious, but without losing its tension and
rich instinctive life. 'From then on it is so to say ready to
jump and projects itself at the first opportunity, namely
when a female person makes an impression which breaks
down the barriers of the commonplace. . . . In the
experiences of a man's love life the psychology of this
archetype is revealed in the form of boundless fascination, over-estimation and delusion or in the form of
misogyny with all its degrees and varieties, which cannot
be explained at all by reference to the real nature of the
particular "objects". . . . In a case of Anima projection one
might define this figure as the sum of all the contents and
qualities which remains over if the real person of the
beloved is subtracted from the total picture which the
lover has outlined in his mind. This sum constitutes an
autonomous complex in the unconscious of the subject,
which is ready at any time to produce a new projection.'[2]
The tragedy which is painted in the brightest colours in

[1] Gustav Schmalz, *Einige Bemerkungen zur Praxis der Psychotherapie*, in the
Zentralblatt f. Psychotherapie, X (1938), p. 144.
[2] *Über den Archetypus, Zentralblatt f. Psychotherapie*, IX (1936), p. 271.

literature or cynically caricatured and which lurks
behind this process is revealed to the doctor.

The experience of the Anima cannot be produced at
will since it is a matter of coincidence, fate and guidance.
All that one can do is to be prepared for the adventure
which such an experience always represents and to set
aside all idea that it is something bad, sinful and un-
manly. One must also not be disheartened by the thought
of having to investigate the relationship and realize it,
though a strong and powerful tendency urges one to do
so. Concretizing the relationship is not the task of
instincts and obscure impulses but of the reflective mind,
which should become master of the passion and guide it.
But to attain its throne the mind must come to terms with
the whole range of the archetype. All artificial self-
control and hyper-masculine ignoring of it, all hiding
behind allegedly religious considerations represents an
evasion of this task which is set by life itself. The Anima
and its energies are thereby repressed and it slips back
into the unconscious. This attitude which is apparently
so 'reasonable' and is sometimes garnished with a touch
of asceticism, very often departs from the archetypal
bases of the laws of life. The revenge which consciousness takes is, according to the particular psychic con-
stitution, either a stunted personality or a neurosis, as in
the example of the officer which we have quoted. The
Anima makes itself evident in dreams and fantasies as a
female figure, and it was this that first led to the discovery of this complex. The neurosis is also from the
angle of depth psychology a desire for healing on the part
of the psyche. It expresses a desire for a return to the
bases of the laws of Nature, which had become buried in
the collective unconscious. Some people, however, can
endure the loss of the Anima in the consciousness: they

are built on a larger scale; above all, younger people in the middle of life intent on success. 'After the middle of life a constant loss of Anima means an increasingly serious loss of vitality, flexibility and humanity.' Such people seem 'soulless' but the animation, that is, spiritualizing, of this sphere of life invests the personality with a 'soul'—which is why Jung uses the term 'Anima'. The clear-cut task is to attempt to come to terms with the Anima, in a way corresponding to truth and reality. Education should show the way. Mortification and repression are an escape; the all-important thing is to look the power of the Anima complex squarely in the face and to get to know it, then it will lose its danger and can be taken possession of by the mind and made part of it.

It is of the utmost importance to understand the mechanism of projection. Through a pre-conscious vital process an unconscious content belonging to the subject is transferred to the object so that it appears to belong to the object. The Anima function is projected. 'But the projection ceases the moment it is clearly recognized, that is, when it is realized that the content actually belongs to the subject.' This has often happened collectively in history. The polytheistic heaven of antiquity lost its influence when its figures were unmasked as a mere reflection of human types. The figure of the Grace was seen to be a representation of erotic fantasy and the witch the image of human intrigue. But these very human characteristics disturb the dreamer and the neurotic as archetypal images.

Even they depend, therefore, on the attitude in which the Anima is constellated. The power and fascination which seem to proceed from the object, from a man or woman, as a result of projection, must be experienced in all its strength and influence, but, and this is the most difficult aspect of the task, knowledge of the projection must slowly permeate the feeling. That which dominates, attracts and arrests the lover in the object in fact proceeds from himself, is inside himself. This transposition will succeed the more easily if the first step in the process of individuation has already awakened suspicions against mere appearance and given cause to take spiritual reality seriously. It is useless to repeat the facts of the projection to oneself purely intellectually: the important thing is the inner experience. It will be some time before the real facts become part of one's innermost feeling and it takes time to see the objectivity of the other person. The projected contents gradually fall back on the lover himself. But there is danger in this 'introjection'. The ego must be immediately differentiated from the contents that have been taken back. A real technique is necessary to attain the 'objectivation of the Anima'.[1] One may ask: 'What do you want of me?' There is an advantage in putting the question to the Anima so personally. Its 'personality' is thereby recognized and the possibility of entering into relationship with it is established. The more personally it is regarded the better. 'The art consists in giving voice to the invisible *vis-à-vis*, putting at its disposal the mechanism of expression for several moments, without being overwhelmed by the disgust which one may naturally feel with oneself at such an apparently absurd game, or by the doubt in the "genuineness" of the voice of the *vis-à-vis*.' What do you want, what are you aiming at, what pleases you so well? one will ask oneself. The fear of foundering in mere feeling must be resisted. One must practise the art of speaking to oneself from an emotion, as if the emotion itself were speaking. As long as the emotion lasts, criticism should be withheld. But if the

[1] *Beziehungen zwischen dem Ich und dem Unbewussten*, pp. 139ff.

emotion has 'presented its case' then the mind must contend with it critically just as if it were confronted by a 'real and friendly person'. Question and answer must succeed one another until the result of the discussion is satisfactory. 'Whether the result is satisfactory or not is decided by the subjective feeling. It is naturally useless to humbug oneself. Scrupulous honesty towards oneself and no hasty anticipation of what the other side may say, are indispensable conditions of this technique of education of the Anima.' Another factor makes the process more difficult. Anyone who tries to abolish the projection of his Anima in this way will not only experience the most intense feelings of love, the joy and happiness of well-being, he will also be suddenly thrown into the opposite emotions. Indignation and bad temper towards himself and the whole world will make him unbearable. As a neighbour in the house of the soul the Anima has all the good and bad qualities of a fellow lodger. One naturally puts the blame on one's own behaviour for being so 'unnatural'. But one must know that when a projection is annulled the archetype breaks up into its own opposite. Everyone can imagine what the opposite of the Anima contains if he thinks of various husbands at home and the way they treat their relations, or of bachelors. The technique of objectivizing the Anima helps us to differentiate ourselves from it. The usual rule is the outright rejection of these unpleasant tendencies as a weakness of our own.

They are not our own striving but are forced on us by the unconscious, i.e. by the Anima. The falling asunder of the opposites when a projection is annulled irritates us violently at first, for the soul is steering between Scylla and Charybdis, between pleasure and displeasure, love and hatred, confidence and suspicion. The same process

will play an important part in our discussion of the archetype God. It ought not to be concealed that the technique
that has been described so unemotionally here involves a
period of the most painful spiritual conflict for the
subject. The whole soul aches as if it had lost all its
protective skin and yet it feels that whilst an illusory
solution would bring relaxation it would bring no real
solution. The heart burns like a wound, but this very
pain has to be suffered to the bitter end, honestly and
objectively, that is, without either courting it or evading
it. Admittedly, most people only notice that a projection
of their own spiritual energies existed when love grows
cold or is disillusioned by a tiresomely commonplace
action on the part of the real object. This too shows how
difficult it is to become detached from a projection. The
ego finds itself between hammer and anvil. The archetypal situation is like a forge. The invisible masterpiece
would be the personality. It is the intermediary between
the demands of the outside world which are reflected in
consciousness and the needs of the inner world which are
imaged in the archetypes of the collective unconscious.
The powers from outside and from within waver round
this centre. They are related to one another like opposite
poles which must meet at the centre. The tension between
them gives birth voluntarily or involuntarily to a middle
'sense'. This is a kind of final court of appeal in the soul
which is difficult to define, 'one has a feeling of what one
ought to be and might be. To deviate from this presentiment means taking the wrong path, it is the way of error
and disease.'[1] Jung thinks that if it did not have such
powerful religious associations he would use the term
'conscience'. This word would 'describe this court of
appeal excellently'. We shall discuss this further later on.

[1] *loc. cit.*, pp. 131ff.

The change in the personality can be illuminated still more by a different metaphor. The soul is like a large country. The struggle with the archetypes, in this case the Anima, is a voyage of discovery into unknown territory with all the dangers, troubles and fears bound up with such an enterprise. Will the 'ego' be able to take it on and withstand it all? It can shut its eyes to it, escape or put up immovable boundary posts. Then a swamp bereft of all conscious culture will develop in the unconscious. A vital problem will have failed to have been solved. But the ego can also take the risk of marching in, entrusting itself to the unknown and—losing itself. 'She half pulled him in, half sank he down.' For this happens when man succumbs to the first onslaught of the feelings and puts them into action. The only way that is worthy of a human being is exploration and spiritual appropriation, that is, cultivation and control. Admittedly, the ego returns changed; inwardly broader, better informed and sustained by an inner feeling that is expressed in a premonitory knowledge of the breadth and depth of the soul, of its brightness and darkness. From now on this 'knowledge' influences every deliberate decision: it is a conscience. It says to the ego: You must now take this new province into account and incorporate it in your behaviour; its voice is like that of a secret, invisible adviser. Jung describes this feeling as the new and slowly developing centre of the personality. Its centre is no longer in the ego, as the sum of the contents of consciousness but in a point between consciousness and the unconscious. Jung calls it the Self. In the above diagram this 'process of centring' is illustrated by the arrows which point to the Self. Individuation aims at the formation of the Self, which is why it can also be called the 'development of the Self' or the creation of the self. But

the road to this goal is still a long one. For with the
'yoking' of the Anima (in woman, of the Animus) only one
province has been conquered, only one part of the soul
centred on the self. Many further strokes of the
hammer have to follow in the forge of life. Behind the
Anima complex land appears. The struggle with it and
its objectivization merely opens up a way to the depth of
the collective unconscious, as experience in analysis
shows. Again, there are two kinds of encounter with the
collective psyche: 1. Through the archetypal situation.
In this situation man experiences the effect of an archetype on the basis of external circumstances even if he
does not realize it or gives it another name. 2. Artificially, through analysis. This led Jung to an understanding of the inner processes and made it possible to
clothe them in words. Let me describe both ways.

One sometimes meets men and women of great
serenity, inner clarity, wisdom and goodness. They have
experienced much and have had to fight a hard fight
through life; usually they work in a community. It is not
knowledge that makes them great and admirable; even a
completely uneducated peasant can penetrate into the
unknown depths. One has a feeling that their real home
is elsewhere; a mysterious magic surrounds them and
influences their environment. How have they become
like this? To discover the reasons one has to read the
wrinkles on their face and look into their unfathomable
eyes. They tell of the hard fate that they have defied and
with which they have wrestled: in family life; in responsibility for wife and child; in concern for a community;
in grave personal temptations; in defeat and bitterness of
heart; calmly endured victory; illness and mortal peril;
the treachery of others; the consciousness of leadership;
the knowledge of the secret forces of history and the costly

experience of the relationships which bind one age to another; the discovery that the individual only represents a link in the chain of cause and effect, but a link which includes the possibility of freely conscious and dangerous deeds. And not least a struggle to discern the meaning of the Whole, to discover whether it is immanent in the world or whether it can only be discovered when man surrenders by a conscious decision to a transcendent 'unknown' power, of which he is the creature. That is the problem of God. All that is easily recounted; but young people only glimpse what is behind it when they meet such secret kings. Such men and women, who have grown to wisdom, have very rarely considered the psychological development of their personality. Jung's psychology has provided the insights and concepts with which the inner process can be expressed in words. But the theoretical expression in words and concepts is, again, understandable only on the basis of similar personal experiences of one's own. That is a condition which is forced on us by the object of psychology, 'the soul'. The phenomena in question lie 'for the most part beyond the frontiers of merely medical knowledge', in fact they are beyond the frontiers of mere intellectual knowledge altogether. They embrace a sphere of 'universal human experience'. A psychology that derives from real life and influences real life can no longer appeal exclusively to an 'intellectual, scientific point of view', it must also take into account the emotional aspect of life. In opposition to the facts of real life this aspect has often been very largely eliminated and suppressed. The peculiarity of the way of individuation described here derives from the fact that everything the soul contains is included, incorporated. 'And there is above all the fact that we are always conscious that what we are concerned with in this kind of practical psychology is not the human soul in general but individual souls in the present age, with all the modern problems that afflict us all directly. A psychology that merely satisfies the intellect can never be a practical psychology, for the whole of the soul can never be grasped by the intellect alone.'[1]

It should have become clear in the description of the first way to personality—the way of the archetypal situation—that it is not a question of the will or the mind but of the total staking of the whole of one's life, and this is at the same time a natural process of separation: 'But under all circumstances only those people attain a higher degree of differentiation who are called and destined from the very beginning, that is, who have an urge and a capacity for higher differentiation, wherein, as is well known, people are extremely varied. ... Nature is aristocratic.' Aristocratic, not, however, in the sense of descent and talent, for 'in order to pass through a far-reaching psychological development it is not necessary to have special intelligence or other talents, since in this development moral qualities can supplement the deficiencies of intelligence'. This process of personality-formation lasts throughout life. Life itself 'analyses' man, which is why it has been suggested that life itself should be termed, somewhat bombastically, 'the Eternal Analysis'.[2] Only death brings it to an end. Death is the final archetype. Those who have survived an otherwise fatal situation have often felt that the experience was an enrichment. It may be said that it has long been known that personality is moulded by life. That is quite true but Jung has taught us to appreciate the inner circumstances and has clothed the process in words. He took the second

[1] *Das Unbewusste im normalen und kranken Seelenleben*, pp. 164ff.
[2] Kranefeldt, in C. G. Jung, *Wirklichkeit der Seele*, p. 272.

way, his experience in analysis, as his starting-point. The treatment of neurotics revealed the spiritual processes more clearly and acutely. But the insights he acquired can be applied to healthy spiritual life as well. The normal process of individuation leads through the archetypal situation. Jung's psychology teaches us how to take this path consciously. Knowledge of his research gives a sense of security and a view of one's own development. Knowledge of the relationships between life and the maturing personality is also a help in the guidance of souls.

The *second* way to the development of the self is the way of analysis. In so far as a neurosis provides the opportunity for psychotherapeutic treatment it is the necessary way for the soul in question. But here too the doctor can only accompany to the extent that the urge for conscious control manifests itself. Answers are not understood by a man if the questions or the possibilities of such questions have not been awakened in him. But if there is in the patients, and that includes not only neurotics but also those who are searching for the meaning of life and have not made any progress, if such people are prepared for a higher form of consciousness, then the collective unconscious will be activated by analysis. The same thing happens in the training analysis which young psychologists and therapists undergo from a serious thirst for knowledge and in order to be of help to others. The frontier opens according to the stations of the Persona, of the personal unconscious and of the Anima and a vista of unimagined grandeur, splendour and terror is opened up.[1] All the archetypes which were constellated above by the situation of life and needed a whole lifetime to penetrate and be assimilated all suddenly flow into the terrified consciousness as archetypal images in fantasies.

[1] *Seelenprobleme der Gegenwart*, p. 335.

'One is involved in aimless experience and judgement with all its categories has travelled impotently to hell.' O. A. H. Schmitz has described such experiences in his *Fairy Tale from the Unconscious*.[1] In the Introduction Jung writes that whoever receives such experiences, comes to know the soul as something objective, as a spiritual non-ego. 'This experience is like the discovery of a new empirical world. The supposed vacuum of a merely subjective space is filled with self-willed objective forces and is revealed as a cosmos to which the ego also belongs in a transformed guise. The great experience involves a shattering of the foundations, a revolution in our presumptuous world of consciousness and a cosmic shift in our outlook, the nature of which we are still quite unable to grasp or even perceive intellectually.'[2]

Thoughts and feelings appear in persons who speak and act; moods are expressed by landscape pictures and instincts clothe themselves in animal figures. As a totality they represent a 'vivid portrayal of all the activities of life' in images. We can guess at the danger of the situation when all these contents of the soul are activated by analogy. For with the archetypal images there are connected emotional values such as we have become familiar with in the projection of the Anima. Hence too the fear of becoming too absorbed in oneself. But 'to have a soul is the hazardous enterprise of life'. Long before Jung's discoveries became known a lone and misunderstood researcher, Ludwig Staudenmaier, had conjured up in himself the 'vista' and the experience of the archetypes. He was a theologian and scientist at the episcopal High School for Girls in Freising. He came face to face with many archetypes, heard them speaking clearly

[1] Munich, 1932.
[2] Introduction to O. A. H. Schmitz, *Märchen aus dem Unbewussten*. Cf. also Johannes Kirschweng, *Odilo und seine Geheimnisse*, Freiburg, 1941.

and saw them in action. Among the fantasy figures I would especially mention the 'goatsfoot' as the personification of the devil. The soul appeared to him as a sum total of contradictory complexes, which act autonomously as 'part-souls'. If the ego were to lose its security and be controlled and swallowed up by them, its attitude to the outside world would be unhinged, which would be equivalent to a psychosis. Staudenmaier paid for this constant struggle with a ruined nervous system. He died forsaken in Rome and embittered—a condition to which the lack of appreciation of the contemporary world had contributed. But his book *Magic as Experimental Natural Science*[1] which was written with the necessary self-criticism gives us a slight idea of the oppressive experiences which stream through the psyche when the collective unconscious is activated. Many 'visions' and experiences of the saints as reported in their biographies also belong to this category. An examination[2] of the reports of St. Antony's temptations has proved that the so-called demonic phenomena were purely psychic in origin and content. The devil invaded Antony in human and animal form, a multiplicity of demons with horrible grimaces. One has only to think of Gruenewald's representation of the devil on the Isenheim Altar. A prostitute brought in by the devil caused Antony serious temptations. On the basis of scientific, religious and cultural analysis the saint's demonic experiences have been shown to be hallucinations. These hallucinations were caused by obsessions and demonophobia. As far as the obsessions and phobias are concerned, they were an expression of 'the heightened sensitiveness of the cortex which results from the weakening and

[1] *Magie als experimentelle Naturwissenschaft*, Leipzig, 2nd edn., 1922.

[2] Josef Stoffels, *Die Angriffe der Dämonen auf den Einsiedler Antonius*, Theologie und Glaube, II (1910), pp. 721–732, 809–830.

exhaustion of the organism by strict asceticism, fasting and
vigils in connection with strenuous contemplation'. The
contents of the phobias, the demons, ghosts and voices,
are attributable to the 'demonological sphere of ideas
that frightened men's minds in Oriental monasticism'.
This is a sphere of ideas 'which was very apt to promote
the rise and strengthening of demonological phobias and
obsessions'. At this point, however, the treatise is out of
date from Jung's point of view since one can now ask,
with him, what was the cause of the fear of demons and
ghosts? Was the belief in demons an invention, a purely
temporary explanation of unknown natural phenomena,
or did it not rather originate in the language of the background of the soul? The demonic experiences of many of
the saints are like an artificial activation of the collective
unconscious. The biographies of the saints are a rich
source of psychological information on the collective
unconscious.[1]

The Anima appears in the shape of the prostitute or
temptress. The figure of the devil is also important: the
figure that worried St. Antony as well as Staudenmaier
and which appears in almost all the biographies of the
saints. It should not cause any surprise that the devil and
the woman become blurred and are consumed in a fog of
visions, although they were conveyed so concretely and
vividly by the saint. The test would be to fast in a hot
climate for forty days, with prayer and meditation, absorption in God, the world and sin, a kind of heightened
spiritual exercise. The mind would become dizzy, the

---

[1] To be able to differentiate genuine demonic from purely psychic
phenomena requires the gift of 'discerning the spirits'. But the collective
unconscious is involved even in genuine demonic occurrences; for—if one
may make a conjecture—the demonic powers take possession of the images
of the archetypes which exist in the soul and work through them. The
reason for this assumption is the similarity between, in fact, the identity of
the images and phenomena.

frontiers blurred. In such conditions man is no longer able to distinguish himself from the fantasies which invade him from 'above' and 'below'. The experimenter will regard his fantasies as real—as though he were in a fever. They are in fact real but only in the psychic order. The devil and his paramour are archetypes of the collective unconscious.

The poets are able to provide a further insight into the secret depths of the collective unconscious and its contents. It is his own depth which is the creative element in the artist, not his constructive mind: at any rate this is what distinguishes the genuine poet from the hack writer. Jung has examined the effects of great works of art, particularly in the drama. When a 'typical situation' is represented it takes hold of the audience, they suddenly feel themselves liberated or upheld, or transported by an overwhelming force. In these moments man is addressed not as a single being but as a generic being. The voice of humanity sounds inside him. 'It is like the bed of a spring of water dug deeply into the soul where the life that formerly spread with groping uncertainty over wide but shallow surfaces suddenly plunges into a mighty flood when it reaches that particular concatenation of circumstances which have contributed from time immemorial to the producing of the primordial image. The moment in which the mythological situation enters is always characterized by a special emotional intensity; it is as though strings in us were being touched which had never sounded before, or forces were being unleashed of whose existence we had no inkling.'[1]

The experience of the collective unconscious acts in exactly the same way, only spontaneously from within: 'Every contact with the archetype, whether it is

[1] *Seelenprobleme der Gegenwart*, pp. 70ff.

experienced or merely spoken, is "moving", that is to say, it acts, for it releases a stronger voice than our own. Whoever speaks with archetypes speaks as if with a thousand voices: he moves and overwhelms. At the same time he raises what he describes from a unique happening into the realm of constant being, he elevates the personal destiny to the destiny of humanity and he thereby releases in us all those helpful forces which have always enabled humanity to rescue itself from all danger and to endure the longest night. That is also the secret of the effect of art.'[1] Thus the great poets provide us with information about the depths of the soul. Their figures are real images of the world and at the same time 'condensations of inner images which express the life and being of the soul itself'. The archetypes which are experienced when the collective unconscious is opened up by analysis stand in the same relation to the outward situation of life. Inversely, knowledge of the collective psyche makes it easier to understand modern poetry. Music also fits into the wide framework of 'complex psychology'. At the same time it can be seen from all these signs that the phenomena of the collective unconscious have always been well known to the initiated and the wise. They have translated the primordial images of the soul into the language of their own age, thereby enabling the seekers to have access to the deepest sources of life.

In addition to Staudenmaier's book, the temptations of St. Antony and works of art, the Oriental books of wisdom give some idea of the 'vista' which presents itself when the collective unconscious is artificially activated by analysis. The consonance extends so far that, except for the stylistic characteristics of different nations and different ages, the pictorial representations of the

[1] *loc. cit.*

Oriental way of wisdom are identical with the drawings which have been produced by the patients of Jung and other psychotherapists during analysis and the process of individuation.[1] But comparison with Staudenmaier and the saints also shows that the artificial activation of the collective unconscious is an abnormal way and an interference with a development of the spiritual life which is by nature slow and unconscious, and which should follow the pace of the archetypal situation. Just imagine all the problems, tensions and conflicts which Peer Gynt experienced in the course of his anything but short life— imagine them all pouring down on a man and crowded into the one or two years of a psychotherapeutic treatment. In the dialectical process with the doctor it is a matter of coming to terms with all these vital problems. It is easy to see what a responsibility the analyst thereby takes upon himself.

The task is always the same: the struggle with the uncanny power from the depth. The Indian Yogi must resist the enticements and threats of the deities and demons; the saint resists the devil and his paramours, and modern man strives to free himself from the 'embrace of the unconscious'. The technique of differentiating the ego from the collective unconscious comes into its own. The ego has to defend itself against two dangers. One is the identification with evil which would result in an inflation full of uncanny influence on consciousness. The second danger to which one almost always succumbs to some extent is 'that one admires oneself a little for having looked more deeply than others'. One regards oneself as significant and extraordinarily influential on others. To put it archaically, one feels like a magician equipped with

[1] Cf. the illustrations in *Das Geheimnis der goldenen Blüte*; in *Das tibetanische Totenbuch*; in the *Eranos Yearbook* 1934; and in G. R. Heyer, *Organismus der Seele*, Munich, 1932.

mysterious powers. The coming to terms with the Anima
and the other archetypes causes changes in the 'energetics
of the soul'. The autonomous complexes lose their
significance, they lose their potency. But where does the
free energy get to, who burdens himself with the factor of
autonomy, significance and extraordinary influence?
The obvious danger is that the ego will lay claim to it.
Then it will assume the rôle of the 'strong man in the
form of the hero, the chieftain, the magician, the medicine man and the saint, the lord of man and spirits, the
friend of God'. The equivalent in woman takes a feminine form: 'It is a superior motherly figure, the Great
Mother, the universal goddess of Mercy who under-
stands and forgives everything and has always desired
the best, who has always lived for the others and never
sought her own, who is the discoverer of the great Love.'[1]
According to Jung, the same psychological factor of a
charging with energy that does not belong to the ego is
the meaning of Christ's statement: 'I and the Father are
one.' He calls that a 'powerful confession' containing 'a
terrific ambiguity'. The factor of significance which is
conveyed by the liberated energy is still condensed in an
archetype. Jung calls it the 'mana personality'. Mana is
the autonomous value of the assimilated complexes. It is
expressed in the feeling of being full of occult and
mysterious powers. According to this interpretation,
Christ merely identified himself with the mana
personality.

The spiritual striving and intellectual penetration of
the problems expressed in the images, connected with a
deep experience of joy and grief in the darkest solitude,
take the change of personality further, as it was initiated
by the assimilation of the Anima. It is perceived as a

[1] *Beziehungen zwischen dem Ich und dem Unbewussten*, pp. 186ff.

'change in the inner feeling', as if all the resistant forces, all the opposing spiritual complexes were being brought into line with a centre which does not lie in the ego. A kind of ulterior consciousness is felt. The ego gradually feels itself as one complex among others, that is, it only knows that it is that and it takes its bearings accordingly. Seen as part of the process of individuation this is the result of the activation of the collective unconscious, different variations of which have been shown above. Consciousness and the unconscious confront one another. The assimilation of the unconscious signifies a *rapprochement* between the two halves. Their centre lies between them and no longer in consciousness, as experienced hitherto. The new centre is the centre of the 'total personality', it provides a 'new balance'.[1] The central position of this 'perhaps virtual' point between consciousness and the unconscious provides a new and firm foundation. Jung realizes the novelty involved in speaking of a 'centring of the total personality': 'I admit of course that such visualizations are never more than clumsy attempts of the mind to express inexpressible, scarcely describable psychological facts. I could say the same thing in the words of St. Paul: "But now I do not live but Christ lives in me"(!). Or I could refer to Laotse and appropriate his Tao, the Way of the Centre and the creative centre of all things. What is meant is the same in all these cases. I am speaking here as a psychologist with a scientific conscience, and from this point of view I am bound to say that these facts are psychic factors of indisputable influence, not the inventions of an idle mind, but definite psychic events which obey quite definite laws and have their regular causes and effects, which is why we can prove their existence among the most varied nations

[1] Cf. the diagram on p. 124.

and races today as well as thousands of years ago. I have no theory about what these processes consist of. One would have to know what the psyche itself consists of to be able to answer that question. For the present I am content to state the facts.'[1]

The process of individuation advances slowly but steadfastly. The tensions and opposites fade and alternate, and the Self is born, the goal of individuation. Insoluble problems lose their urgency as a higher and wider interest arises on the horizon. The problems from which one suffers are not solved logically but simply fade out in the face of a new and stronger direction in life. Nothing is repressed or made unconscious but everything simply appears in a new light, and therefore becomes different: 'What on a lower level had led to the wildest conflicts and to emotions full of panic, viewed from the higher level of the personality now seems like a storm in the valley when seen from a high mountain top. This does not mean that the thunderstorm is robbed of its reality; it means that, instead of being inside it, one is now above it. But since, with respect to the psyche, we are both valley and mountain, it seems a vain illusion if one feels oneself to be above what is human.'[2] The strength of the emotion is felt even now, one suffers, is shattered and tormented. And yet everything is different. Something in the soul is no longer inside pain, but beyond it. And this is the deepest place where one is quite alone with oneself. And this ulterior unknown takes the emotion as its object and can say: 'I know that I suffer.' Jung calls the new consciousness which is slowly formed the 'Self'. It is felt as something irrational, as an 'indefinable existence'. The ego is distinct from it,

[1] *loc. cit.*, p. 175.
[2] Introduction to *Das Geheimnis der goldenen Blüte* (*The Secret of the Golden Flower*), pp. 21ff.

precisely because it is felt to be beyond consciousness. But the ego adheres to the Unknown; it rotates round the Self like the earth round the sun. The connection between them, the ego and the Self, cannot be known. The word 'feeling' characterizes the perceptual character of the relationship. Therefore nothing can be said about the contents of the Self. The ego feels itself to be an object, a part of an Unknown and superior Self. There is no proof of the existence of the Self. But it is a postulate that is justified by psychic phenomena. 'It is as though the conduct of life's affairs had passed to an invisible central authority.' The appearance of this feeling almost always brings a solution of spiritual complications. The personality is released from emotional and intellectual entanglements. A unity of one's whole nature is experienced which is felt as a liberation. Jung uses the term 'divine' to describe the peculiar mode of the experience of the Self and its influence. The goal of individuation is the 'original Christian ideal of the Kingdom of God', that is 'within you'.[1] This centre of the personality is the 'God within us'.[2] St. Paul is full of this liberating experience: 'it is the consciousness of being a child of God which redeems us from the curse of the blood. It is also a feeling of reconciliation with events in general.'[3] How does Jung come to connect the psychic feeling of the centre of the personality with the concept of God? Has he forsaken his starting-point, psychology, or does he degrade God into a spiritual fact? It is now necessary to examine his conception of God. In his language that is at the same time the archetype God.

[1] *Beziehungen zwischen dem Ich und dem Unbewussten*, p. 183.
[2] loc. cit., p. 203.
[3] Introduction to *The Secret of the Golden Flower* (German: pp. 70ff).

CHAPTER THIRTEEN

RELIGIOUS EXPERIENCE

THE contents of the collective unconscious are, in their totality, a natural view of the world as it has coalesced and combined in the course of human history. During our journey through the land of the psyche we have often met God as an important constituent of this image of reality. If God had not been encountered in this context as a spiritual fact which can be experienced directly, He would never have been referred to at all since, Jung writes, natural science has not discovered a God anywhere and epistemology proves the impossibility of knowing God but the soul comes forward with the assertion that it has had a direct experience of God.[1] This inner experience of God is 'valid in itself'. It therefore needs no proof of a non-psychological kind. It is also beyond the scope of any form of non-psychological criticism. As the most direct and most real of all experiences it cannot be laughed away and cannot be proved not to exist. 'The ideas of the moral law and of the Godhead are part of the inextinguishable substance of the human soul. Therefore any honest psychology which is not deluded by a philistine arrogance must grapple with these facts. They cannot be explained away or dismissed with irony. In physics we can do without the concept of God, but in psychology the concept of God is a definitive factor which has to be reckoned with as much as emotion, instinct, mother and so on.'[2] God and the religious disposition in man are psychologically

[1] *Seelenprobleme der Gegenwart*, p. 384.
[2] *Über die Energetik der Seele*, p. 180.

effective and therefore real. Jung even calls them the
strongest and most original of all man's spiritual
capacities.[1] The psychologist and the psychotherapist
have to reckon with the reality of the soul if they want
to cure its diseases. 'Many neuroses are based primarily
on the fact that, for example, the religious demands of
the soul are no longer perceived, owing to a childish
belief in rational enlightenment. The contemporary
psychologist should know by now that religion is not
merely a question of belief in dogma but an attitude
which is a psychic function of almost inconceivable
significance.'[2] Jung refuses, however, to trespass beyond
the frontiers of his discipline; the scope of his judgement
is confined to the effective activities of the soul. 'It does
not behove psychology, as a science, to undertake to
hypostatize the image of God (=the archaic image of
God). Psychology merely has to reckon with the function
of the image of God, in accordance with the actual
facts.'[3]

Jung shows how this objective approach to religious
problems works out by taking the problem of the
immortality of the soul. Psychology offers a 'natural
proof' for the immortality of the soul. The results of
telepathy have shattered the idea that the psyche is
dependent on the brain. Hitherto it has not been possible
to invalidate the theory that consciousness is limited by
space and time. Every penetration of the barriers of time
and space is therefore of fundamental importance. The
phenomena of telepathy show that spatial and temporal
limitations of the psyche can be wiped out. 'If anyone
were from the necessity of his innermost heart or in
accordance with the age-old wisdom teaching of the

[1] *Wirklichkeit der Seele*, p. 65.
[2] *Seelenprobleme der Gegenwart*, p. 105.
[3] *Über die Energetik der Seele*, p. 159.

human race or from the psychological fact of the occurrence of telepathic perceptions to draw the conclusion that at bottom the psyche participates in a form of being beyond time and space and therefore belongs to what is inadequately and symbolically called "eternity", his critical reason could offer no opposing argument except the scientific *non liquet*.[1] But the person who denies this is 'isolated against the eternity of Nature in his embrace of reason', for it is the nature of souls that speaks in the religions. Most religions are systems of preparation for death. The two greatest religions, which survive today, Christianity and Buddhism, see the meaning of existence in its end, that is, they prepare man for life beyond death, since, according to their teaching, the soul is immortal. Religions are, however, the antithesis of rational speculation, they are not the product of cogitation; according to Jung they are 'natural revelations of the soul of humanity'.[2] From this it follows that 'whoever does not conclude that the soul is immortal, out of scepticism or rebellion against tradition or lack of courage or superficial psychological experience or thoughtless ignorance, is very unlikely to be a pioneer of the spirit and quite certain to fall into conflict with the truths of the blood'.

The patient must sometimes be told that his image of God or his conception of immortality is suffering from consumption and that his 'spiritual metabolism is therefore out of hand'. 'The old pharmakon athanasias, the remedy of immortality, is more meaningful and deeper than we thought.'[3] Above all, people who have passed the middle of life face the problem of seeking the meaning of life. The quest for outward success and victory is over,

[1] *Wirklichkeit der Seele*, p. 229.
[2] *loc. cit.*, p. 220.
[3] *Seelenprobleme der Gegenwart*, p. 274.

old age is beginning. Life's vital energies turn within, to the inner world. The psychotherapist has to lead the patient in the way of spiritual hygiene and help him to conquer the inner world. If in the first half of life the archetypal foundations have been ignored in the ambitious quest for success and the 'instincts' and the 'truths of the blood' disregarded, nature will very likely be avenged now in the form of a neurosis, an inner breakdown or painful awareness of meaninglessness. The neurosis is often concealed under the most harmless looking symptoms. Only one way leads to a recovery of health. 'Absolutely complete life is possible only in harmony with them (the archetypes), wisdom is a return to them.'[1] In broaching the problem of God it is therefore primarily a question 'neither of faith nor of knowledge, but of an agreement between our thinking and the primordial images of our Unconscious . . . and one of these primordial ideas is the idea of a life beyond death'.

Jung derides those who are not satisfied with that. 'There are unfortunately many feeble minds who thoughtlessly imagine it is a question of truth, whereas it is really a question of psychological necessity.'[2] Jung follows the religious needs of the soul, the greater or lesser desire for conscious faith, and he thus avoids the question of truth. He allows some patients to slide back into the protective bosom of Mother Church. 'I am firmly convinced that a vast number of people belong to the fold of the Catholic Church and nowhere else, because they are most suitably housed there.'[3] They then continue to live in a state of partial unconsciousness since the Church with its dogmas and rites takes over

[1] *loc. cit.*, p. 273.
[2] *Über den Archetypus*, p. 272.
[3] *Die Beziehungen der Psychotherapie zur Seelsorge*, p. 29 (= *Psychotherapists or the Clergy*, p. 282) (*Modern Man in Search of a Soul*).

the task of steering the spiritual forces of the archetypes into safe paths, so that, if they follow the commands of the Church, they come through life without being ship-wrecked. They are spared the ordeal of grappling consciously with life, but they are denied the experience of the Self.

Jung leads those who do not suffer a relapse along the path of individuation and allows them to mature into the experience of the Self. This final phase of individuation must now be described in greater detail. Anyone who has at some time been conscious of the abyss of religious doubt in his soul, can more or less assess what it means to try and find one's way through the chaos within, single-handed and free from all ties. One is responsible solely to the ego. Is it strong enough to bear the burden? 'The shirker experiences nothing but a morbid fear which brings forth no meaning.' But the steadfast fighter experiences a transformation within himself, he feels the concentration of all his spiritual energies and instincts and in the process the ego arrives at a peripheral position. The goal of this process is obscure to begin with; all that can be established is its significant effect on the personality. But the fact that the whole feeling of life is intensified and life remains in flux indicates the 'peculiar appropriateness' of the change. The new centre of the psyche is felt to be a point of suspension of all tensions; it is outside them and yet it embraces them in a peculiar way. It unites them in a centre. Something like pure life, pure psychic energy can be felt there. This quite unique feeling may appear as a symbol in the pictorial representation of the dream or vision. It is the 'reconciling symbol' which occupies a privileged position among the wealth of possible symbols. It unites within itself all the psychic energy which lives

in the opposites, which is capable of transfusion and combination and it represents the seat of creative energy. All
spiritual energy finds its adequate expression in the
ultimate and supreme symbol, the unifying, all-com-
bining symbol. As an authentic symbol it transcends all
rational understanding; it is the expression of the
creative activity of the soul. In this latter respect the
unifying symbol represents the experience of God. 'As
the expression of this mysterious force, which constitutes
the basic essence and being of man, the vision of the
image of God and of its antithesis is connected with the
symbol of energy.'[1] It is a 'glance into the depths of
the divine soul'.[2]

The following vision was seen by a woman patient by
intensive concentration on the background of consciousness and after long training. It represents the birth of
her self and at the same time her individual conception
of God. Jung recounts it in the patient's own words:

'I climbed up a mountain and came to a place where
I saw seven red stones in front of me, seven on either side,
and seven behind me. The stones were flat like steps. I
tried to lift the four stones nearest me. In doing so I discovered that these stones were the pedestals of four
statues of gods buried upside down in the earth. I dug
them up and arranged them about me so that I was
standing in the middle of them. Suddenly they leaned
towards one another until their heads touched, forming
something like a tent over me. I myself fell to the ground
and said, "Fall upon me, if you must! I am tired!" Then
I saw that beyond, encircling the four gods, a ring of
flame had formed. After a time I got up from the ground
and overthrew the statues of the gods. Where they fell,

[1] Toni Wolff, *Einführung in die Grundlagen der komplexen Psychologie*, in
Jung-Festschrift, p. 154.
[2] *Bruder Claus*, in *Neue Schweizer Rundschau*, 1933–34, p. 229.

four trees shot up. At that blue flames leapt up from the ring of fire and began to burn the foliage of the trees. Seeing this I said, "This must stop. I must go into the fire myself so that the leaves shall not be burned." Then I stepped into the fire. The trees vanished and the fiery ring drew together to one immense blue flame that carried me up from the earth.'[1]

For a complete understanding of this unifying symbol the whole context would have to be recounted from which the fantasy is extracted. Jung only gives a few hints: The idea of the centre which is reached by a kind of ascent (mountain climbing = effort, labour). The medieval problem of the squaring of the circle, which belongs to the realm of alchemy, is here a symbolical expression for individuation. The four gods, as the four cardinal points of the horizon, characterize the total personality. They are the four functions which make it possible to find one's bearings in the psychic sphere. The circle encloses the Whole. The conquest of the four gods means liberation from identity with the four functions. With this action, that is, the conscious coming to terms by means of the technique of objectivization there arises an approximation to the circle, to the undivided Whole.

Similar experiences are represented pictorially in the Oriental Mandalas. These are pictures full of splendid colour and symmetry, of the lotus flower, for instance, which is called the 'golden blossom'. Its 'secret' is the symbolical representation of the individualized psyche. Reference has already been made to parallel drawings by Europeans. One inevitably compares them with the visions of the mystics in all times and places. Hildegard

[1] *Relations between the Ego and the Unconscious*, p. 220. (trans. by R. F. C. Hull in *Collected Works*, Vol. 7, Routledge).

v. Bingen appears to have felt intensely a unifying symbol, or rather, its influence. Jung quotes her as follows:

'Since my childhood, I always see a light in my soul, but not with the outer eye, nor through the thoughts of my heart; neither do the five outer senses take part in this vision. . . . The light I perceive is not of a local kind, but is much brighter than the cloud which bears the sun. I cannot distinguish in it height, breadth or length. . . . What I see or learn in such a vision stays long in my memory. I see, hear, and know at the same time and learn what I know in the same moment. . . . I cannot recognize any sort of form in this light, although I sometimes see in it another light that is known to me as the living light . . . while I am enjoying the spectacle of this light all sadness and sorrow disappear from my memory.'[1]

Jung himself knows a few people who have personal knowledge of this experience. Some unifying symbols from the early Middle Ages are universally familiar, e.g. Christ in the centre and the Four Evangelists or their symbols at the cardinal points. He also mentions the Heavenly Jerusalem with the exact description of its symmetry in the Revelation of St. John. St. Teresa built the citadel of her soul in a similar way. The blessed Brother Nicholas von der Flue in Switzerland originally saw a terrifying menacing vision full of wrath and concentrated energy. It became the centre of all his thought and further visions. In six equal circles he entered the most significant mysteries of the Faith around this centre, so that the whole picture really became a 'symbol' (symballein = throw together) of the content of his life.[2]

[1] *The Secret of the Golden Flower*, trans. by C. F. Baynes, p. 104 (Routledge, 1931).
[2] Cf. Alban Stöckli, O. M. Cap., *Die Visionen des seligen Bruder Claus*, Einsiedeln-Cologne, 1933. Also Jung's commentary: *Bruder Claus*, in *Neue Schweizer Rundschau*, 1. Jahrgang, 1933–34, pp. 223–229.

Even Christ Himself can become the unifying symbol. According to Jung, Paul expresses this in the words: 'I live, yet not I, but Christ lives in me.' As a unifying symbol, Christ the 'corner-stone' is at the same time the stone of wisdom in which everything is contained.[1] That alone is the reason for the influence of Christianity: 'The apparently unique life of Christ has become the hallowed symbol because it is the psychological prototype of the only meaningful life . . . of a life which strives to attain the individual, that is to say, the absolute and uncon- ditional realization of the law peculiar to itself. In this sense one may speak with Tertullian of *anima naturaliter christiana.*' The deification of this Jesus of Nazareth is not surprising either, since it affords a striking proof of the honour in which humanity holds this hero. He remained faithful unto death to the inner law which was inborn in Him. Therefore He is the supreme example of the process of becoming a personality.[2] On the other hand, it would be megalomania to imagine that the white man Christ is the only Redeemer! Jung places Buddha alongside Christ.

In Jung's psychotherapy, therefore, the goal of re- demption is God. But *this* God is *in* the soul and to confirm his view Jung quotes from Master Eckhart: 'God must for ever be born in the soul.'[3] God, in Jung's view, arises in man through individuation. 'We must direct our patients to the place where the One, the All- Uniting arises in them.' All the forces of the soul are concentrated in the Self, the soul is made 'whole'—that is redemption according to Jung's theory of the soul. 'The journey through the spiritual history of mankind has the purpose of restoring man as a whole by rousing

[1] *Erlösungsvorstellungen in der Alchemie*, p. 9.
[2] *Wirklichkeit der Seele*, p. 202; *Psychologie und Religion*, pp. 159ff.
[3] Introduction to *The Secret of the Golden Flower*.

the memories of the blood.' Complex psychology sees its significance in restoring the connection in the total psychic structure between the unconscious and consciousness, in healing the soul, making it whole: a problem which in periods of collective culture devolved on the redemptive religions, but which today, as the logical termination of the line of development initiated by Protestantism, must obviously be solved by and in the individual.[1] The individual must face his own religious problem, that is, the problem of giving birth to the expression of his own supremely personal nature in the unifying symbol of the Self. 'But our soul is strong enough to create new religious forms and symbols —not artificial, collective and universally valid symbols but individual symbols, which do justice to the variety and character of the individual. From this point of view our age is only at the beginning of a new spiritual culture.'[2]

In its consequences Jung's complex psychology leads therefore to a particular attitude to all the problems of the Cosmos. It intends that the Self should know as a direct inner experience 'what keeps the world together at its innermost centre'. 'Thus there results from the experience of psychic reality a particular view of life. It is not a philosophy, since it explains neither the world nor the spirit, and it is not a religion, for it cannot say anything about the metaphysical. At the most it may be called a particular philosophical attitude based on psychological facts which have been proved trustworthy and valid; or a religious attitude, insofar as man has come to see that the ego is not the final court of appeal,

[1] Toni Wolff, *Einführung in die Grundlagen der komplexen Psychologie* in *Jung-Festschrift*, p. 48.
[2] *Seelenprobleme der Gegenwart*, p. 431.

but that it is enmeshed in helpful and destructive powers, which extend beyond its capacity and comprehension and to which it must expose itself.'[1] Jung's teaching claims to provide the bricks and the tools with which everyone can build his own conception of the world, culminating in the individual experience of the Self as the true redemption of the soul. This is the salvation to which man aspires. For this condition is felt to be higher than the former one, 'in fact as a kind of redemption from compulsion and similar responsibilities'. St. Paul expresses this sense of liberation and redemption in the consciousness of being a child of God. Man redeems himself and the world appears to divide into itself with no remainder, like an identical equation!

[1] Toni Wolff, *Einführung in die Grundlagen der komplexen Psychologie*, in *Jung-Festschrift*, p. 167.

PART TWO

CHAPTER ONE

RELIGION

CRITICISM of Jung's position must concentrate on two clearly distinguished aspects: the philosophical presuppositions and the psychological research. Only a clear disclosure of the philosophy and its background will permit an objective appreciation of the psychological research, by freeing it from its more or less conscious presuppositions and integuments. Jung himself writes: 'Presuppositions are inevitable, and since they are inevitable, one should never pretend that one has none.' What exactly is Jung's attitude to metaphysics and religion? Jung interprets the experience of the Self as an experience of God, with the aid of metaphysical concepts and terms which he adapts to the methodical level of psychic experience. How does he justify this?

'A new philosophy of life must reject all superstitious belief in its objective validity, it must be able to admit that it is only a picture that we paint to please our own soul and not a magic formula with which we posit objective things.'[1]

According to this, a philosophy of life is merely an extension and deepening of consciousness. This means, however, that all our thinking, knowing and feeling about the meaning of our existence is mere psychology. 'It is really my purpose to push aside, without mercy, the metaphysical claims of all esoteric teaching. Secret motives of gaining power through words are in ill accord with the profound ignorance which we should have the

[1] *Seelenprobleme der Gegenwart*, p. 332.

humility to confess. It is my firm intention to bring into the daylight of psychological understanding things which have a metaphysical sound, and to do my best to prevent the public from believing in obscure power words. . . . To understand metaphysically is impossible; it can only be done psychologically. I therefore strip things of their metaphysical wrappings in order to make them objects of psychology. In this way I can at least get something comprehensible out of them, and can avail myself of it. Moreover, I learn psychological conditions and processes which before were veiled in symbols and out of reach of my understanding . . . my admiration for the great Eastern philosophers is as great and as indubitable as my attitude towards their metaphysics is irreverent. I suspect them of being symbolical psychologists.'[1]

In the old psychology it was beyond all doubt that the overwhelming being of God was a person with a will and consciousness of his own. He was the quintessence of all reality. Jung explains that his position is quite different:

'The concept of God is a necessary psychological function, irrational in its nature, which has nothing at all to do with the question of the existence of God. The intellect can never answer this ultimate question, still less can it provide any proof of God's existence. In any case such proof is entirely superfluous, for the idea of an all-powerful divine being is present everywhere, if not consciously, then unconsciously, since it is an archetype. Something or other in our psyche has superior force and if it is not consciously a god, it is at any rate the "belly", as St. Paul says. I therefore think it wiser to acknowledge

[1] *The Secret of the Golden Flower*, trans. by C. F. Baynes, Routledge, 1931, p. 128.

the idea of God consciously, otherwise something or other will become God, usually something very inadequate and stupid; the sort of thing that an "enlightened" consciousness may well concoct. Our intellect has long known that it is impossible to think of, let alone imagine the fact and mode of God's existence accurately any more than the mind can conceive of any process which is not causally determined.'[1]

According to Jung the wisdom teachings of the East are merely stages in the process of development towards a higher human consciousness, in other words, mere psychology. But as such they are also 'intelligible and—thank God—real, a reality with which something can be done, a reality containing possibilities and therefore alive. The fact that I restrict myself to what can be psychologically experienced, and repudiate the metaphysical does not mean, as anyone with insight can understand, a gesture of scepticism or agnosticism pointed against faith or trust in higher powers but what I intend to say is approximately the same thing as Kant meant when he called "das Ding an sich" (the thing in itself) a purely negative border-line concept. Every statement about the metaphysical ought to be avoided because it is invariably a laughable presumption on the part of the human mind, unconscious of its limitations. Therefore when God or Tao is spoken of as a stirring of, or a condition of, the soul, something has been said about the knowable only, but nothing about the unknowable. Of the latter, nothing can be determined.'[2]

'What God is in Himself' is a question beyond the scope of psychology. This implies a positivistic, agnostic renunciation of all metaphysics. It is possible that meta-

---

[1] *Das Unbewusste im normalen und kranken Seelenleben*, pp. 10ff.
[2] *Secret of the Golden Flower*, p. 135.

physical objects have their share of existence, but 'we shall never be able to prove whether in the final analysis they are absolute truths or not'. In saying this Jung clearly stands—as he himself admits—'on the extreme left wing in the Parliament of the Protestant spirit'. One might therefore think of Jung as a positivist since in his view only the natural sciences lead to positive knowledge. But it must be added at once that he has penetrated and extended brutal positivism and fought for the 'reality of the psyche'. He has acquired a new province for empirical knowledge. With a magnificent gift of empathy he does justice to the intrinsic quality of the soul: 'The human soul is neither a psychiatric, nor a physiological nor a biological problem at all, but a psychological problem. The soul is a field on its own with its own laws. The nature of the soul cannot be derived from the principles of other fields of knowledge, otherwise the specific nature of the psychic is violated. It cannot be compared with the brain, nor with hormones, nor with any of the familiar instincts, but for good or ill it must be recognized as a phenomenon *sui generis*.'[1]

Jung sees the reality of the soul, but by his scepticism he closes every path that would lead out of the psychic sphere again. Although he maintains that his attitude is not directed against the belief in higher powers, according to him faith and religion are nevertheless not a bridge to a transcendent world. Jung regards religions as purely natural products of the soul. They are entirely contained within the framework of psychological experience. 'Religions do not derive from the head, but possibly from the heart, or at any rate from a psychological depth, bearing little resemblance to consciousness,

---

[1] *Grundsätzliches zur praktischen Psychotherapie*, p. 79 (= *Collected Works*, Vol. 16: *The Practice of Psychotherapy*).

which is always merely on the surface. They are anything but contrived. They have grown step by step through thousands of years like plants, as natural revelations of the soul of the human race. Religions spring from the natural life of the unconscious soul and give adequate expression to it.'[1] Like a picture book religions tell of the inner world of the psyche, like myths they are projections. 'Dogma is like a dream which reflects the spontaneous and autonomous activity of the objective psyche, the unconscious.'[2] The soul makes religious utterances from its inborn divine creative energy. It 'posits' these essences. How has this come about?

Primitive man saw himself inextricably bound up with all the involuntary forces of Nature. He was one with the universe. This condition corresponds to Paradise. Woe betide the man who dared to rebel against the All-One and, driven by pride, lust for conquest, courage or sheer necessity, touched the 'taboo'. What happened, for example, when he went hunting at a forbidden time of day or year? Did he incur the vengeance of the gods or demons? To begin with he was probably disappointed since there was no sign of good or evil spirits. But he realized that there were chances of success as well as threatening dangers, simply by reason of the unusual circumstances. And both sides of the 'sacrilege' are attributed to his efficiency, circumspection or carelessness. 'The achievement of consciousness is the most delightful fruit on the tree of life,' in fact it is sin itself! The Fall of man in paradise is a symbolical description of the rupture of the unity of man and the world, subject and object. This breaking away from the participation

[1] *Wirklichkeit der Seele*, p. 220.
[2] *Psychologie und Religion*, p. 85.

mystique is the rebellion of Satan. And the parallelism is surprising: 'Ye shall become like God—with knowledge of good and evil.' When the projection is removed, the taboo in which positive and negative, divine and demonic were contained, disintegrates into the opposites of good and evil, god and the devil. Magic develops into religion if the concept of God is purged of the demonic. God and the Devil part company.[1]

To understand this better let us imagine an analogous case: A young boy grows up in the small world of a rural family and later makes up his mind to live his life alone in the frightening but alluring metropolis. He is already regarded almost as a renegade, since the metropolis is 'taboo'. To entrust oneself to it signifies the surrender of all security. But if nevertheless he takes the risk and stakes his life, then the menacing city will soon reveal its two faces: vice and culture. Both correspond, however, to two tendencies in himself and he discovers that both want to attract him on to their side. He is alarmed at the abyss of evil that opens up within him and at the same time he senses the high dignity of all human nature in his yearning. That is the end of a projection; he has taken in parts of his soul which were outside. His consciousness is enlarged. In the same way humanity had to struggle for whole millennia to gain the world. But to the extent that man broke away from his magic, psychic dependence on the surrounding world, the projections were taken back and the spiritual forces disintegrated into their opposites, and man faced the problem of securing himself against these powers, instincts, weaknesses, tensions and antitheses. He needed guidance in his intercourse with the secret forces of the

[1] Leopold Ziegler, *Überlieferung*, p. 252.

soul, gradual initiations into their proper use, safety devices and aids. They were systematized and, according to Jung, that is what our present religions are. 'The total life of the collective unconscious has been as it were completely absorbed in the dogmatic archetypes and flows like a subdued river in the symbolism of the Church year.' 'It was not a speculative philosophy that led to the foundation of Christianity, but an elemental need of the masses who were vegetating in spiritual darkness.'[1] In a symbolical form religions are an image of the collective unconscious. 'My attitude to all religions is therefore a positive one. In their teachings I recognize the figures which I have met in my patients' dreams and fantasies. In their morals I see the same or similar attempts which my patients make from their own invention or inspiration to find the right way to deal with the powers of the soul. The sacred rites, the ritual, the initiations and asceticism are extremely interesting to me as constantly changing and formally varied techniques of producing the right way.'[2] Man as a collective being 'invented' the techniques and passed on his experience from generation to generation. The various religions are therefore an expression of humanity's collective experience. Their language is symbolic. The symbol combines the two aspects of the soul, the unconscious and the conscious. On the one hand it is a translation of the primitive expression of the unconscious and of its archaic contents into the language of consciousness. Therefore the symbol arises from the deepest being of the soul. On the other hand, as an Idea corresponding to the highest presentiments of consciousness, it is also an expression of the individual's spiritual achievement. Both sources flow

[1] *Wandlungen und Symbole der Libido*, p. 68.
[2] *Seelenprobleme der Gegenwart*, p. 81.

together and 'throw' (*symballein*) their contents into a compact image. The symbol is an expression of both halves of the soul.

God is a symbol of the overwhelming impulse of the soul to goodness and joy, and at the same time an expression of the supreme yearning of the soul for redemption. The devil is a symbol of our own abysmally deep wickedness and the fear of consciousness of the superior power of evil. God and the Devil both live within us, they are an antithetical pair, two poles which need one another. God cannot live without the devil—in our soul. Hence the warning of the specialist in spiritual hygiene that we should not close our eyes to evil and repress it. That would mean secreting the evil from the compound of good and evil which we call 'man'. What would remain would, however, not be an angel but, as experience has shown us, a Satan. The directrix for intercourse with the Anima, for example, is represented symbolically by the Church. The Christian is born from 'Mother Church' as from an immaculate divine womb (*ab immaculato divini fontis utero*, as stated in the liturgy for Holy Saturday, which Jung himself is constantly quoting). Thus the Church sets up guiding principles for the Christian's attitude to the sexual and regulates the activity of the Anima complex right up to the contraction of marriage. As the '*Primizbraut*'[1] it even appears as the 'projected expression' of the Anima. The sacraments are 'wise and appropriate' initiations into man's use of his full unconscious abilities. Confirmation as a form of dedication represents the gradual breaking away from parents; marriage is the binding of sexual

[1] '*Primizbraut*' is a small girl, dressed like a bride, who offers to the newly ordained priest a small bridal crown. The Church (as the bride) offers herself as a virgin to the priest (representing Christ as bridegroom) to be married.—*Translator*.

relationships. The Mass is a resurrection charm, for daily reorientation and protection. And absolution, the sacrament of penance, provides for the return to the normal way. What Jung here applies to the Christianity of the Catholic Church can be extended to all other religions. His view is therefore that the various religions are therapies and systems of salvation and healing for the diseases and disturbances of the soul,[1] 'methods of spiritual hygiene'.[2] They are ways of salvation which promise to accompany the faithful traveller to his life's end without too much spiritual peril. Therefore humanity is well looked after by its religions.

Now comes the great BUT. The development and differentiation of the human soul was stimulated above all by the Enlightenment. But the various religions stood still and became torpid. Externally they had found an ideal and ritual form in which all the hopes and strivings of the soul are received and expressed. But the advancing differentiation of the soul soon outgrew the range of 'the local religions of the West' and the existing forms of religion were no longer capable of embracing the whole fullness of spiritual life and the soul was left to its own devices. The Church no longer meets the soul with understanding. It speaks another tongue, it has different problems and different feelings. The soul begins to become a factor which cannot be compassed by ordinary means. 'The various religions have lost their absolute validity, because they no longer satisfy the advanced differentiation of consciousness, that is to say, they do not embrace all the components of consciousness. Therefore they are no longer able to express symbolically the whole complexity of the psyche and their *gratia*

[1] Introduction to *Das Geheimnis der goldenen Blüte*, p. 64.
[2] *Psychologie und Religion*, p. 81.

medicinalis has become ineffective.'[1] Of the modern
development and refinement of the spiritual forces we
may particularly note an intensification of the consciousness of personality, a more clearly marked feeling for the
concrete and the particular, a stronger development of
the sense of responsibility. The differentiation of the
modern consciousness develops the individual. The long
years during which there has been a discrepancy between
the leadership of the Church and the new stage of consciousness has led to a sceptical reaction against religion;
men have lost their faith and have been thrown back on
themselves in their intercourse with the forces of the
soul. 'Because of this scepticism modern consciousness is
thrown back on itself, and as it flows back subjective,
spiritual phenomena are rendered conscious, which
were always present, but lay in the deepest shadow so
long as everything was able to flow smoothly outwards
(projected on to the symbols of the Church).' Twentieth-
century man has thus been deprived of all the metaphysical certainties of medieval man.[2] What man did
with his free spiritual energy and how he found his way
about is to be seen clearly in art with all its 'isms, which
are only intelligible psychologically.[3] For many people
there can be no return to the dark womb of Mother
Church since 'the spirit of this age demands moral
autonomy'. The way of conforming to and confiding
blindly in the collective symbols of the Church 'is too
much in contradiction with the intellect and its rational
morality, for us to be able to regard this solution of the
problem as exemplary or even possible for us at all. If

[1] Toni Wolff, *Einführung in die Grundlagen der komplexen Psychologie*, in
Jung-Festschrift, p. 53.
[2] *Seelenprobleme der Gegenwart*, p. 412.
[3] Cf. the essay on Picasso in *Wirklichkeit der Seele*, pp. 170ff.

on the other hand we think of the figures of the Unconscious as collective-unconscious dominants, and therefore as collective psychological phenomena or functions, this does not clash in the slightest with our intellectual conscience. This solution is also acceptable on rational grounds.'[1] In our age the man of high moral and intellectual standards no longer wants to follow a faith or rigid dogma. He wants to understand and to know, he wants to have the first-hand experience for himself. He wants to plunge down into the soul for himself and to get to know its powers, including its religious powers and then express them symbolically, in accordance with his own individuality. This means that 'private' religion, not collectivized religion, is the way out of the lack of religion in our age. The future belongs to the formation of religions of an individual nature.

Jung deliberately leads his patients to individual religion as the way of salvation, that is to say, the way of individuation with the Self as the goal.[2] The experience of finding the Self is redemption. It is connected with a subjective, redeeming feeling of great luminosity. An overriding sense of purposefulness inspires all the energies of the soul which are concentrated on the centre of the personality. 'If one summarizes what people tell one about their experiences, it comes more or less to this: They came to themselves, they were able to accept themselves, they were able to reconcile themselves with themselves and they were thereby reconciled to unfavourable circumstances and events. This is practically the same thing as used to be expressed in the words: He has made his peace with God, he has sacrificed his own

---

[1] *Das Unbewusste im normalen und kranken Seelenleben*, pp. 143ff.
[2] Cf. the example which is described in detail in *Psychologie und Religion*, pp. 117ff.

L

will by subjecting himself to the will of God.'[1] That kind of experience moves in the same direction as the process of flowing into the Indian Nirvana. This latter is not an empty Nothingness, but pure life emptied of all illusions. The individual life is merely a mode of expression of the general and complete life. But awareness of 'being involved in a deeper and wider life' is redemption. It is experienced by incorporating one's own purpose in life with the 'great impersonal purpose'. The solitary way to the innermost personal Self is the realization of the inner meaning of one's life. It is not a blind alley leading nowhere, not a self-abandonment in the wilderness, since at the end of the way of individuation something new appears. In the greatest solitude the fullness of being appears which is perhaps expressed in consciousness in the feeling that one's personal existence is justified. The condition we have described is, according to Jung, the 'Kingdom of God' within us, the Divine. 'The psychological fact that has the greatest power in a man acts as God, because it is always the overwhelming psychic factor that is called God.'[2] There is therefore a reciprocal relationship between God and man but it is such that 'on the one hand one can conceive man as a function of God and, on the other, God as a psychological function of man'.[3] God is immanent in the soul. 'It is the soul that makes metaphysical assertions from its inborn divine creative power,' the soul 'posits' the differences between the metaphysical essences. 'It is not merely the condition of metaphysical reality, it is metaphysical reality.'[4] Consequently, the various religions only give information about the mysteries of the soul; they are a symbolical

[1] *Psychologie und Religion*, p. 147.
[2] *loc. cit.*, p. 146.
[3] *Psychologische Typen*, p. 340.
[4] Introduction to *Das tibetanische Totenbuch*, p. 19.

expression of the process of individuation and lack all the qualities of a supernatural revelation. They lead man to the sources of life in his own soul—unfortunately unconsciously. Prayer, the sacraments, the following of the Commandments, meditation, Bible reading are all merely exercises towards the attainment of spiritual equilibrium, spiritual hygiene, mere psychology. The Yogi and the Buddhist submits to the same measures to maintain his 'spiritual metabolism'. Religions are—in brief—symbolical psychologies! The science of comparative religion offers the best evidence for this assertion. Jung describes the psychological background against which comparative religion introduces its figures. His researches allow him to draw a conclusion based on the results of comparative religion, namely, that the parallelisms and common features of all religions and popular traditions are the expression of the one soul of the whole human race. The differences between the various religions are a proof of this in themselves since they demonstrate the dependence of the soul on environment, climate, soil and national tradition. Each nation seeks after God; the various religions are expressions of the different ways that lead to Him. All of them are true but restricted to a particular human group. 'Race, nation, and culture are different vessels in which even divine truth assumes different forms.'[1] What is the meaning of 'divine truth'? What is the kernel beneath the many different shells? If we remove the husks of the various religions, what remains is the autonomous, purposeful, one might almost say, absolute, life of the psyche as the divine ground. The key to an understanding of the symbolical psychologies is very simple. The

[1] Keller, *Analytische Psychologie und Religionsforschung*, in *Jung-Festschrift*, p. 292.

assertion of a 'transcendent' existence in the metaphysical sphere merely means a mode of existence 'trans-
cending consciousness' and must always be translated thus.
Metaphysical objects only belong to the unconscious part
of the soul. 'Unconcerned about time-conditioned, philosophical pros and cons, a scientific psychology must think
of those transcendental views which have arisen in the
human mind at all times, as projections, that is to say,
psychic contents which have been put out into metaphysical space and hypostatized.'[1] All assertions about the
other world, the world beyond, the Kingdom of God, grace
and miracles, are projections of unconscious spiritual contents. All the relevant sayings of Scripture and the symbols
and institutions of Christianity can be explained 'naturally'.

The psychological interpretation of religious assertions
is particularly obvious in such quotations from the Bible
as 'I live, yet not I, but Christ lives in me'. According to
Jung, this expresses a feeling of being a child of God, in
other words, a psychic fact, the experience of the Self.
In the statement 'I and the Father are one' Jung interprets the reality of the Father psychologically and ranks
it with the empirical experience of the Mana-personality
which represents a dominant of the collective unconscious and with which the Son identifies himself. In the
language of science this thinking of Jung's must be called
psychologism, the levelling down of supra-psychic
realities to the level of purely psychic reality.

But more important than Jung's interpretation is the
fact of the discovery and exposition of the Self, which
cannot be denied the 'status of a religious experience'.[2]
It is moreover a fact that this discovery helps many
people to live, for a time at least, since they experience

---

[1] *Ueber den Archetypus*, p. 264.
[2] *Psychologie und Religion*, p. 108.

the numinous in themselves. Individuation releases man's natural religious predisposition from the dross of centuries of so-called 'enlightenment' and awakens it from the torpor of the dormant psyche. In addition, however, by providing the key to the interpretation of the symbols and images of the Self Jung has made possible an insight into the nature of this predisposition. The unified, centred psyche expresses its religious life in the unifying symbols which are the equivalent of the mandalas with which the Orient has made us familiar. The fascinating effect of these experiences of the Self, which are felt to be 'the most overwhelming psychic factor', is an indication of the preciousness of the 'psychic material', the preciousness which is appropriate to an image of God. The psyche which tastes itself, acquires a taste for this 'breath', for the 'spirit' which modern man has had to do without through centuries of so-called 'enlightenment', so that it is not surprising that this unfamiliar feeling often has the attribute of the 'divine' bestowed on it. Man is now preparing to re-discover the psyche and its world; he is exploring the land of the soul, enriched by all the discoveries of science, so that he can see through every projection and avoid all hypostatizing; but burdened with a scepticism which denies all reality to the supernatural world. This has psychological results of which it is difficult to forecast the ultimate effect. For—and here Jung's own weapons are turned against him—the human psyche is an organism in which all the parts act and react on one another. Just as an unconscious tendency forces the senses to make typical slips, so that attitude of the highest part of the soul, the intellect, the 'eye of the soul' (Augustine) has an influence on the life and experience of the psyche. Different metaphysical views are bound to have a different effect on the organism of the soul and be reflected in the experience of the soul. Metaphysics opens a man's eyes to realms above and the self-experience of his psyche will be differently constituted in such a man than in one whose scepticism has closed the 'eye of the soul' with a bandage and which forces it to look exclusively within. Jung himself observed such differences when he compared the unifying symbols of his patients with the mandalas of other ages and nations: 'A modern mandala is the involuntary confession of a particular spiritual condition. There is no deity in the mandala, and no subjection to or reconciliation with a deity is indicated. The place of the deity appears to have been taken by the totality of man.'[1] The psyche is isolated from the world 'above' and enclosed within itself as in a hot-house; all its energies are powerfully concentrated on the inner life and the fruit is a changing flood of self-creations in a splendour of images such as only the living psyche can produce. Flowers always grow a more brilliant hue in a hothouse than in the open air. The flowering and growth of the self-enmeshed psyche is the individual religion of modern man, a kind of 'natural mysticism'. Depth psychology opens up new depths into man's absorption with himself.

At the same time there is the new problem of distinguishing between Christian mysticism and the kind of 'natural' mysticism we have just described. A comparison of the visions of a St. Hildegard of Bingen with the mandalas of the Indians and of modern Europeans would inevitably shed light on mankind's religious potentialities in general and the potentialities of the Christian religion in particular. The solution of this problem will require a great deal of material showing the differences between the dreams of Christians and non-Christians.

[1] *Psychologie und Religion*, pp. 147ff.

CHAPTER TWO

ANTHROPOLOGY

FROM the Enlightenment right up to the latest manifestations of rationalism the nature of man has been
seen as a purely intellectual, rationalistic reality.
The soul has been equated with consciousness. The ego
is the most concentrated expression of the nature of man;
the basic stratum of man coincides with the ego's sphere
of influence. All attempts to interpret the nature of man,
from Descartes to Leibniz and Hegel, have one thing in
common. They have 'an idealizing quality and are related
a priori to a rational view of human nature'.[1] This
extreme rationalism of the last few centuries has led to an
equally strong reaction—an example of the law of compensation which is also operative in the collective sphere.
Nature in man revolts against the intellect. The instinctive, obscure, impulsive element cries out for consideration and recognition. The vital energies confront the
sphere of consciousness, Bios confronts Logos, or to put
it in psychological terms, the unconscious confronts consciousness. In the anthropological-philosophical research
of the period which has been described as an 'anthropo-
logical turning point',[2] the relationship between Logos
and Bios has turned out to be a 'concentration point'.
The main concern of the present 'doctrine of man' is to
study the part occupied by the system of natural instincts
and needs within human nature as a whole and to
explore its influence on the whole of human life. The

[1] Friedrich Seifert, *Die Wissenschaft vom Menschen in der Gegenwart*, Munich,
1930, p. 11.
[2] Friedrich Seifert, *Zur anthropologischen Wende in der Wissenschaft*, in
Blätter für deutsche Philosophie, Vol. 8, 1934–35, p. 403.

recognition of the full reality of man in the duality of
Logos and Bios, mind and spirit, intellect and instinct
(consciousness and mere existence), 'West' and 'East',
consciousness and unconsciousness, was the first step in
the revolution in the view of human nature which set in
at the beginning of the twentieth century. It now became
a matter of exploring the relationship between the two
parts of the human soul. The fact that their relationship
was interpreted dualistically can only be explained by
the law of historical reaction. Freud rediscovered the
earthy depths of human nature, but his sexual theory did
not lead to the liberating incorporation of the unconscious in the totality of human nature. He reduced it to
the category of the morally bad.

In the same way Ludwig Klages based his conception
of man on the conviction that there is a fundamental
antithesis between Logos and Bios, consciousness and the
unconscious, mind and soul. He regards man's remote-
ness from all instinctive immediacy as the decisive cause
of every kind of spiritual trouble. According to Klages,
man is suffering from an excess of consciousness. The
conscious 'mind' is the enemy from the very outset. It has
robbed the 'soul' of its innocence, it desires knowledge
and the power to discriminate, and it was thus that the
first sin occurred. The Biblical story of Paradise is the
deepest allegory of the basic truth of anthropology as
understood by Klages. In the Fall man tore himself away
from the maternal arms of Nature. That is the meaning
of man's mourning for Paradise Lost. Man yearns to
return to Paradise, he must return there. The way back
leads via a 'dionysiac sympathy, a magic at-one-ment
with the chthonic forces', to the ultimate restoration of
the state of nature. This will involve a merging of man
with the impersonal life of the Cosmos, a return to the

womb of Mother Nature, which will change man into a pure 'bearer of life'.[1] Then he will be a pure living creature, but no longer a spiritual person. This is one of the results that flow from the biocentric view of life. Fundamentally it is a biological caricature of man. Klages represents the extreme reaction against the modern cult of consciousness.

C. G. Jung, however, is not subject to the law of historical reaction. He has broken with the preconceived idea of the dualism between Logos and Bios and has advanced towards a synthesis; he has found the 'middle way'. He affirms and accepts both mind and spirit, Logos and Bios, consciousness and the unconscious. He transforms the conflict and antithesis into a complementary relationship and seeks to reunite the intellect with the laws of the unconscious. He is therefore opposed to Freud's materialistic reduction of the unconscious and is the absolute opposite of Klages. He does not want to return to a 'second naivety', but requires a higher consciousness. A life that is bound up with the spirit and a spirit that is just to the claims of life is guaranteed by the mutual fertilization of Logos and Bios.

But—and here a question may be permitted which may well arise as we study Jung's works—does the interplay of thought and life, Logos and Bios, consciousness and the unconscious, really do justice to man's deepest nature? Does not one get the impression that man is the defenceless victim of the tension and interaction between the two sides of his nature? 'Is it the final truth about man that his whole being is subject to the polarity of Nature?'[2] Is there any room for freedom in Jung's system, is freedom of decision eliminated? In other

[1] Cf. Hans Pfeil, *Der Mensch im Denken der Zeit*, Paderborn, 1938.
[2] Friedrich Seifert, *Die Wissenschaft vom Menschen*, p. 33.

words, is man only a link in a natural chain, is he merely a living creature, albeit equipped with consciousness, or is he a spiritual person?

On close examination it is clear that in the dialectic process of curative treatment Jung does not in fact appeal to consciousness, to the ego. He wants to make contact with a third factor, through the ego. He speaks to an unknown third element in man. The patient is told to face a danger calmly; but whence does consciousness derive the power to resist the danger? A patient is told to observe his depression; who takes the initiative and sees that the ego is able to wrest from itself the power to let sombre feelings come up quietly? Jung attaches the greatest importance in the curative process to the 'living through' of previously unconscious material. Interpretation and rational explanation will not bring this about. What is required is rather that consciousness should in its own way take an active part in the 'marriage' with the contents of the unconscious. Is there a third element which is situated neither in consciousness nor the unconscious but stands above the parties and on which true leadership devolves? The psychotherapist's whole effort must be concentrated on wooing and alluring this third element until it is born and becomes the clear centre of the soul. This element is what Jung calls the 'Self'. The law of polarity requires a third force which stands above the opposite poles and embraces them both. The spell of natural polarity is broken as Jung proceeds from duality to triplicity. The power to take free decisions in matters of spiritual development is inherent in this mysterious new element, the Self. This is the place where the regular flow of tension is broken and a new layer of being appears. It connects the psychic process with something above the natural sphere. This place sustains the highest in man, it is the seat of his spiritual personality. It follows that as a psychological scientist Jung strives unintentionally towards a 'personalistic conception of man' with the empirical material of the psychotherapist. In Jung's conception of man the freedom of the spirit comes to light in the Self.

Clear though Jung's personalist view of man is when one surveys his work as a whole it is less evident in the details of his work. One often feels that the freedom and power of the spirit are stifled and crushed to death by his naturalistic psychology of polarity. There is some justice in this reproach but it needs to be modified. The spiritual personality in man is part of a stratified structure. Underneath the spiritual upper layer powers are at work which influence and even direct all the activities of knowing and willing and all creative thoughts and images. Anyone who divagates from the 'centre' is aware of this inexorable law. But Jung has derived what he calls the laws of life from the spiritually diseased and thereby clearly demonstrated the dependence of the highest stratum in man on its natural foundation. In spite of this, it is possible to argue that something of the real nature of man does survive in Jung's teaching, as compared with the theory of a purely naturalistic psychology.

One would, however, like to see more of the essential nature of man preserved in Jung's psychology. For example, his description of the phylogenetic origin of the archetypes does not seem to do justice to the nature of the human person. Has he not applied a purely naturalistic theory of evolution here? The process of the transfer of the original libido to an analogy of the object of the instinct may be seen correctly by Jung, and also the binding of the transformation of psychic energy to

symbols which then appear as archetypal images. They
are like the power station which imitates the waterfall.
But must not the power station be there first? Must there
not exist in the soul a predisposition or a readiness for the
alteration in the expression of energy? Or, to put it in a
different way, a million masculine experiences of woman
do not create a sexual predisposition. On the contrary,
they presuppose a readiness of mind and body for sexual
experience. The stimulant does not create the predisposition. If a generation in the early life of man was
forced to formulate symbols, the readiness to do this
must have been implanted somewhere in the structure of
the human body and soul. In spite of all the obscurity in
which the laws of heredity are still shrouded, it seems to
be established that what is acquired individually cannot
be anchored in heredity.[1] The question as to how the
agreement between national myths and the products of
the collective unconscious in all times, including our
own, is to be explained, might also be answered by a
reference to the fact that the symbol-forming power of
the human mind has remained constant, only in the
present age it is unused, undifferentiated and repressed
into the background by the cult of consciousness. Nevertheless, Jung's discussion and conclusions on the position
of symbols in man's spiritual life and their connection
with the transformation of energy—and it is in this
sphere that he sees their true value—are an important
contribution to the investigation of symbolism, which is
still an almost entirely unknown territory.

In the present state of knowledge of man there is,
however, more to be said for regarding a basic structure
of body and spirit which is based *a priori* on the 'laws of

[1] Just Günther, *Vererbung*, Breslau, 1927, pp. 114ff; Hermann Mucker-
mann, *Vererbung*, Potsdam, 1932, p. 45.

life' as the source of the archetypes rather than accepting Jung's theory of their phylogenetic origin. And this view of their origin obviates a mechanistic theory of evolution, which would violate the higher strata of the soul. If this view does not actually explain the origin of the archetypes, nevertheless it overcomes the danger of ignoring the nature of man as a spiritual person. A pupil of Jung[1] has dealt with the objection that Jung's theory of the archetypes is based on a materialistic view of man. In reply to the attacks of Oswald Bumke[2] the Zürich school has stated its view of the origin of the archetypes as follows. 'With Bumke we reject the inheritance of acquired experience, but in accordance with the modern theory of heredity we accept that pictorial forms of understanding are bound up with instinctive reactions, are present as hereditary predispositions in hereditary plasma and have developed by means of idiovariation and selection into typical, adapted forms.'

The theory of evolution which Edgar Dacqué[3] has described would fit entirely into the required framework. According to him the predispositions and nature of man were already active in the obscure depths of Nature. The higher qualities were still 'veiled' in the lower, not, however, in any crudely physical state, but so that 'man's total potential was contained in the whole process of organic development' and the organic kingdom represents the unfolding of the basic inner form of man.[4] It makes no difference to the nature of man whether the animal world merely represents stopping places in the process of evolution or man denotes anatomically a

[1] Eva Moritz, *Materialismus gegen Logik und Komplexe Psychologie,* in *Zentralblatt f. Psychotherapie,* XI (1939), pp. 303–317.

[2] Oswald Bumke, *Die Psychoanalyse und ihre Kinder* (Eine Auseinandersetzung mit Freud, Adler und Jung), Berlin, 1938.

[3] Edgar Dacqué, *Natur und Erlösung,* Munich, 1933, pp. 109–136.

[4] *loc. cit.,* pp. 129ff.

foetal condition in animal development. The important thing is that the driving entelechy which has led man to the goal—Dacqué speaks of a 'basic form of man created in accordance with a basic image'—that this was acting from the beginning and bore the nature of man within itself. In this way man is the substantial content of the whole of Nature—*quodammodo omnia*, as Thomas of Aquinas says. The same thing is demonstrated by the contents of the collective unconscious which Jung discovered. Dacqué supports the case for the existence of the collective unconscious by describing myths as dreams of the human race. They are symbols of man's inner experiences in the course of his development. The predisposition to create myths is still present in man today, as is shown by depth analysis. Myths and the fantasies of the analysands which resemble them, are both the expression of a background of the soul which Jung calls the collective unconscious.

It was our concern to show how the theory of the origin of the archetypes can be corrected and incorporated in the new research on primeval history, whilst retaining a personalistic view of man, as against a naturalistic conception of evolution. That is the weakness which Jung's system has in its attitude to the past. Looking forward into the future our concern must be the same: to set forth the image of the human person clearly and distinctly in therapy. And that implies encroaching on the realm of ethics.

CHAPTER THREE

ETHICS

THE stratification of the soul culminates in the Self. Jung describes this court of appeal in psychological terms. It is a ' feeling of what one ought to be and what one might be. To diverge from this presentiment signifies error and disease.' The ego circles round the Self like the earth round the sun. The Self enters into human feeling as something independent and appears on the scene like a secret counsellor. It is an awareness of being part of a deeper and broader life.[1] The Self is as it were the gateway to this new world, in which the inner 'meaning of every human life' is experienced. Not merely known, since knowledge is partial, but experienced in and through life.

Discarding psychological language, the court of appeal which Jung calls the 'Self' might be described as the place where man is open to the universally valid, to the supernatural meaning of life, to the transcendent Truth. It is the innermost point which the mystics call 'the apex of the soul'. It is the place where the Truth speaks to man, so that it may 'sound through' him. It is the place where the personality is actualized. Seen from below, the Self is the organ with which the Truth can be received and with which man comes to see the demands it makes on him, the demand that it should be followed and performed. It is therefore the place where ethical decisions are made. The Self comes close to what ethics calls the conscience.[2] The conscience is 'the organ which receives the eternal challenge of the good that should be

---

[1] *Eranos Yearbook*, 1936, Introduction.
[2] Cf. Seifert, *Die Wissenschaft vom Menschen*, pp. 36ff.

done. The conscience opens man's soul to eternity. At
the same time it directs him into the present, into the
events of every day.'[1] Moral psychology defines the
conscience as 'the function of the whole human personality, in which man becomes aware of the binding
quality of the moral law'.[2] The 'Self' is the psychological
term for this 'function of the whole human personality'.

This brings us to the point from which the relation
between depth psychology and ethics can best be sur-
veyed. Jung's concern is to build the vital energies into
the total human personality. In his own language this
means coming to terms with the contents of the collective
unconscious. It will now be seen how closely fused this
task is with the development of the spiritual centre of the
personality, the conscience. There is an infinitely delicate
and important relationship between the conscious life of
the individual and the ability to be receptive to universally valid truths, to the Good and its demands. Knowledge of this fact has an important bearing on all
educational and pastoral activity. The conscious or
unconscious process of individuation and the formation
of the conscience go hand in hand, each conditions the
other, they influence, promote and disturb one another.
There is a correlation between Being and Knowing,
between what a man makes out of himself, and blindness
or openness to the true and the good, to ethical values.

The association of the formation of the conscience with
the process of becoming a Self must not be based on a
purely biological conception of truth and a purely prag-
matic ethic. If this presupposition were correct, truth and
goodness would develop in accordance with the increasing necessities of life. Truth would be the agreement of

---

[1] Guardini, *Das Gewissen, das Gute, und die Sammlung*, Mainz, 1931, p. 35.
[2] Müncker, *Die psychologischen Grundlagen der katholischen Sittenlehre*, p. 26.

knowledge with human desires and aims, with usefulness and utility. Life itself would contain the principles of goodness; they would not be transcendent. Behind this presupposition there lurks a view of man which regards life itself as the highest value. But that is a misunderstanding of the mode of being of the human person, which finds its principles all ready to hand and recognizes them with the conscience. Jung's ethical discussions would suggest that like Nietzsche he stands 'beyond the true and false, beyond good and evil'. In contrast to the 'old' morality which wanted to see evil completely eliminated, Jung regards good and evil as conditioning one another, they are a pair of opposites in the soul. God cannot live in the soul without the devil! God and the devil are like two poles. It is impossible to take an attitude of 'either—or' and stand exclusively on one side or the other. It is a matter of both the one and the other. The task of religion is to regulate the intercourse between them and maintain a fruitful tension. In the encounter with God and the devil it is therefore not in the least a matter of truth but of 'psychological necessity'.

What Jung has seen are the psychic relates for these factors which are independent of the soul. Between them there is a polar tension in the psyche, owing to which one must not repress the evil in oneself lest it enter into opposition with the good and attack it in the rear in the form of an irresistible tendency which may become as intense as a compulsion. The energetic law of enantiodromia asserts itself with terrifying harshness. The dawning awareness of this terrible law which governs all blind processes 'fills the lower stratum of the modern consciousness with a chilling fear'. Anyone who has experienced this takes the law of enantiodromia into account and learns to differentiate himself from the undulation within himself and he thereby clearly separates the question of psychological necessity, which may first appear in the curative process, from the question of Truth which unhesitatingly follows upon it. Jung's reflections on good and evil, truth and falsehood, God and the Devil have the same significance as for example the question: Should the doctor tell the patient the truth? These are all hygienic matters, mere spiritual dietetics.

But the very respect for the reality of the soul which can be learnt from Jung makes it evident that the human psyche is more than 'psyche', that as a personality it points beyond itself and must make contact with the metaphysical realm because although the patients may 'recover' from their symptoms, they do not obtain peace. They allow themselves to be distracted for a time by the throng of spiritual images and a 'natural mysticism' so long as they cling faithfully to the therapist; but the psyche itself is not healed as is shown by the experience with many patients who wake up out of egocentricity. The spiritual distress of such people shows that a sceptical theory of knowledge fails to do justice to spiritual reality. A psychotherapy which treats man on this basis is necessarily driven to psychologize the qualities of the spirit. But the category of the 'psychic' is not applicable to the category of the 'spiritual'; such a procedure lays itself open to the charge of psychologism. 'If psychotherapy is to be of any further help, it must be supplemented by a therapy based on spiritual values, which is alone qualified to turn to an immanent discussion of philosophical questions and to engage in an objective debate on the spiritual needs of the sufferer'.[1] For the psychotherapist

---

[1] Viktor E. Frankl, *Ärztliche Seelsorge*, Vienna, 1946, p. 15. Frankl calls this necessary extension of psychotherapy—logotherapy.

this means that he can only lead his patients as far as his own Weltanschauung extends.

The result which follows from the psychologistic levelling down of spiritual values in psychotherapy is an ethical attitude which is shadowed in twilight. The patient is exhorted to turn his eyes away from metaphysical objects, to recognize the search for them in an outside world as a projection and to concentrate on the secret growth in the soul itself. A great respect for the individual process of development prevents the therapist from interfering or applying force. The whole art of therapy is intended to make it impossible for the patient to escape into projections: to contain him in his own fire and to make that fire warm his whole personality.

One of the limitations of the therapeutic situation is that the patient observes that he is being 'treated' but not being taken seriously. Above all there are many Christians who fail to progress with their therapist because he refuses to admit the validity of their religious convictions, because he says they are a mere safeguard, an evasion, a support for the person who lacks the courage to stand on his own. The therapist evades the problem of Truth and tries to show that the contents of the various religious doctrines are not the important thing at all: the main thing is whether they have any psychic value. Every religious conversation—and psychotherapeutic treatment leads to such conversations again and again—is shifted from the 'sphere of content to the sphere of action'. The treatment comes to a standstill and the patient begins to feel that the therapist has come to the end of his tether, that he is dodging the real trouble. When the patient feels that way, the treatment inevitably comes to nothing.

Even if we exclude from this chorus those whose

religious education was spurious and whose protest therefore only amounts to a neurotic safeguard, there are still many whose real suffering indicates that there is a weakness in Jung's therapy. The human psyche is more than a spiritual organism the powers of which can be brought into harmony under the medical eye of the therapist. It is true that many people are content with the partial well-being which they call 'health' but spiritually they have been beheaded. The human psyche is a spiritual being which points by its very nature beyond the psychic realm to the metaphysical world. This whole dimension is levelled down by Jung and reduced to the intra-psychic sphere inasmuch as he interprets problems of Truth as problems of psychological necessity. A whole province of the psyche, its supreme province, the 'eye of the soul', namely the intellect, is dimmed and turned inwards with the information that nothing can be known outside the psychic sphere and that the 'Thing in itself' is hidden. This information fences in the eye of the soul: it dare not peep through the holes out of respect for such enlightened knowledge and it resigns itself to the inner vision of psychic images of all the objects which it 'naïvely' presumes are on the other side of the fence.

All healing is expected to come from the process of spiritual growth, from the contact between consciousness and the unconscious, from the development of spiritual individuality in the Self. Therefore Jung's patients are led to revere the psyche and confide in its nature but they receive no guidance from objective truths, objective values and the demands they make. The ego is called on to serve the growth of the soul but it is not confronted with the necessity of deciding on matters of truth. The world of metaphysics is exchanged for the world of the soul instead of their both being united. Jung teaches his patients how to feel at home in the house of the soul but he locks them up in it; the door to transcendence is barred. But the human spirit realizes itself not merely in the process of growth but also in making decisions, since it is a personal spirit. If it is to attain its full development, it must have demands made upon it and that can happen not only as a result of numinous experience, by the extension of consciousness and contact with the original foundations of the unconscious, all of which are necessary first steps, but rather by a call from the transcendent and by an answer given with a full sense of responsibility and self-commitment. In such decisions the person acts and comes to freedom.

That is not to deny that there is a connection between growth and decision, between psychic need and the Truth, insofar as the psyche aspires to be guided by objective principles. It is the art of human culture to lead both spheres to one another, to bring together growth and decision, being and commitment. The nearer they approach and meet, the more man becomes a personality, in the sense of individuation and taking personality to mean 'the person who effects and sustains the good'.[1] But the discrepancy between the two realities will bring a stronger element of exertion and hence a feeling of weakness into consciousness. The will appears on the horizon and demands to be explained. It should be made clear from the very outset that there is no question of a 'dethronement of the conscious mind'[2] in Jung as there is in Freud and Adler, nor of the fear that man's self-determination is in danger. Only the capacity for decision is removed from the sphere of

[1] Theodor Steinbüchel, *Die philosophische Grundlegung der katholischen Sittenlehre*, Düsseldorf, 1938, I/1, p. 351.
[2] Nikolaus Seelhammer, *Die Individualpsychologie Alfred Adlers*, p. 166.

free-will and transferred to the mystery of the Self. This accords completely with what Steinbuechel has to say about the freedom of the will:

'This freedom is one of the most intimate things a man has and can live in. But knowledge has no access to this most personal sphere. Man remains the greatest mystery to himself. . . . Man experiences his own self-determination; but how this becomes possible and actual remains hidden from him.'[1]

Willpower reaches into the very centre of the personality and derives its impulse from that centre, but it is itself embedded in the regular flow of psychic energy within the whole system. Jung therefore defines the will as the sum of energy which is at the disposal of consciousness. In the small sphere of consciousness the will is able to be master. The concept of the soul has been extended by the discoveries of depth psychology and consciousness has been fitted into a wider context. Compared with the great space occupied by the unconscious psyche consciousness represents only a small province; in the same way the sum of energy which is called willpower is tiny in relation to the other spiritual forces. Within the framework of a certain field of action conditioned by temperament and environment these forces unconsciously balance one another and the soul appears to be subject to conscious motives. But when we leave the path of the normal and the path marked out for the individual in advance compensation leads to an opposition of the unconscious forces of the soul to those of consciousness. And in the event of an open conflict, as for example in a neurosis, it will be found that the major part of psychic energy cannot be guided to conform with the will; on the

[1] Th. Steinbüchel, *Die philosophische Grundlegung der katholischen Sittenlehre*, I/1, pp. 407ff.

contrary, it will tend towards the natural gradient and strive to compensate for the difference in intensity, if necessary, by force. This does not involve a denial of man's power of self-determination and freewill. For, as Ignaz Klug has pointed out, 'in the single case everyone can act or refuse to act. But—and this is the crucial point—when it is a question of the total sequence of actions, the chain of actions, what is the position then? Does not experience prove that all our actions spring ultimately from the depths of man's being? They always follow the inner laws of the human structure.'[1] And it is from this bird's-eye view that Jung surveys the way of human life.

The results of this way of looking at life are concerned with the maturing process in oneself and also with the education of others. 'In view of the powerlessness of the will, which is one of the oldest religious experiences, analytical psychology appeals not so much to the will but believes rather in the hidden wisdom of inner growth and the voice that makes itself heard in the process of growth. Inasmuch as like the Oriental wisdoms it speaks of the educational value of passivity and non-interference, it is a necessary reaction against the activism and optimism of Western education which has become very largely an education in the arts of lying and hypocrisy.'[2]

Jung merely mentions willpower and then only to refer it back to its proper confines. Weak though the will is within the total system of psychic energy, another aspect of the will must be mentioned in any critical discussion of Jung's theory of the will, one that also results from experience, namely that the will has a privileged position. Like the index of the balance it can decide the issue

[1] Ignaz Klug, *Tiefen der Seele*, Paderborn, 1926, p. 62.
[2] A. Keller, *Analytische Psychologie und Religionsforschung*, in *Jung-Festschrift*, p. 297.

in the to and fro of the psychic forces, assuming that it is used over a long period within the normal range. Like the steering wheel on a ship it can take the lead when it is used in the right place. But it must be used within the process of a large-scale development. That is why it is so important to gain some insight into the dynamics of spiritual processes which Jung discusses on almost every page of his work. He concentrates attention on the basic process in the maturing of the soul. The will constitutes a small link in this chain if it is working in the right place. All the rest is almost a natural process which has simply to be confided in. This point of view has much in common with Hengstenberg's[1] ascetic theory of pre-decision. He asks what is the process that leads to sinful actions? The action itself merely puts the seal on a development which was initiated by some happening in the soul which took root in man long before the decisive action occurred. Hengstenberg calls this inner process 'pre-decision'. The good pre-decision may be compared to the 'awakening of good opinion'; in the evil pre-decision the seed of sin is sown, it is 'an accomplishment of the human spirit which is known most clearly by our whole personality' which can be grasped from the earliest stage of empirical germination, but not by the reasoning faculty. For it is not rationally conscious in the sense that it flows from some rational consideration. It is true that the intellect is not eliminated, it participates, it is an integral part of the whole spiritual process. 'In pre-decision the whole personality is involved—including heart, mind and will.'

The effect of this spiritual process which takes place in the innermost realm of the personality is far-reaching—for in pre-decisions 'the whole world is changed; it

[1] Hans Eduard Hengstenberg, *Christliche Askese*, Regensburg, 1936.

becomes either light or dark'. It leads to a movement which releases a 'progressive organization of the forces within us'. It is from this inner organization that our actions, good or evil, follow 'explicitly and inevitably'; and our whole future action is traced out in advance. As far as human judgement can tell it leads inevitably to good or evil. The bad pre-decision leads to an enslavement which influences all the other spheres and describes ever wider circles. It influences not merely the will but also darkens the mind. It is 'terribly difficult to escape from the results which flow from such enslavement'.[1] Here, too, as in Jung, very narrow limits are imposed on the will. Attention is concentrated on what happens in the inner core of the personality. It is here, behind the front, that the pre-decisions are made. It is the place which Jung calls the 'Self'. Its birth in the process of individuation clarifies the core of the personality and delivers it over to itself. Thus the will can be used at the right moment to steer the ship although its power is limited. Jung's doctrine of individuation as the synthetic building up of the personality is therefore very important in education. To avoid raising false hopes, it should be mentioned that the application of psychotherapeutic knowledge is restricted by the large assumptions on which it is based. Depth psychology reckons on a good average of spiritual gifts; above all it demands a certain level of intelligence. Where there is a lack of general human ability, all effort will be in vain. In Jung's language there will be no 'appeal to higher consciousness'.

[1] *loc. cit.*, p. 61.

CHAPTER FOUR

EDUCATION

INDIVIDUATION occupies the central position in Jung's theory of education. Its aim is to co-ordinate the various strata of the basic human structure, to set them in order and bring them into line with the mysterious core of the personality which thereby becomes the apex of the human soul. At this point, however, man is open to ethical values. The aim of an individuation which is also intended to be a formation of the conscience is that this insight into ethical values shall function accurately, clearly and cleanly: in other words, objectively. Thus psychotherapy and Christianity meet both in the education of the self and in the education of others. Above all, Jung's theory is important for the self-education of the adult. One fact shows the importance Jung attaches to the task of self-education: the question which has emerged from his thirty years' experiences as a maxim and guiding principle is: 'In what task in life has this person failed?'

Depth psychology shows how much our actions are influenced by unconscious desires. The process of individuation is the way out of a false subjectivism and a world of appearance into the real world, the objective world. What the decisions of conscience are then founded on is no longer 'that egotistical tangle of personal desires, fears, hopes and ambitions, which must be compensated for and corrected by unconscious personal counter-tendencies, but a functional relationship which is related to the world, which places the individual in absolute, binding and indissoluble communion with the world'. The way that is marked out is fourfold:

Self-education begins with disillusionment. To begin with, knowledge of the 'Persona' is necessary. Man is enabled to see his ego accurately and to investigate the principles that guide him in his intercourse with the outside world. The purified ego enters into relationship with the Thou. The I–Thou relationship is animated by the Anima-function. It contains the fullness of all the possibilities of a loving relationship to the world. When a young person enters into relationship with a Thou of the opposite sex for the first time, he is usually left on his own; but this is just the time when advice would be most useful. Warnings alone, which merely point to the dangers, will meet with no response and that is understandable since the whole of life is at stake, it is a venture from which no one can be freed unless he neglects the duty he owes to his own maturing personality. The only thing he is prepared to accept is instruction based on confidence in the goal which is grounded in his own nature. Jung's technique of 'objectivizing' the Anima provides a lead. It develops through the stages of transference, withdrawal and introjection and the conscious coming to terms with the sexual sphere, leading finally to stability and control. Knowledge and experience of the mechanism of projection is inconceivably important since it alone makes it possible to view the happenings in the soul as a whole. A decision of the conscience will turn out differently according as to whether one is irrevocably abandoned to a transference and therefore to the fascinating influence of the Thou, or whether one has recognized the projection and tries to recognize the 'objective reality' of the partner in the transference. A courageous endurance and assimilation of the sexual feeling is necessary, otherwise there is a danger of repression. What results this working on one-self produces may be seen from what happens when failure in this task occurs:

'Its results are the loss of vitality, flexibility and humanity. Usually what ensues are premature sclerosis, if not calcification, monotony, fanatical one-sidedness, stubbornness, pedantry or the opposite, resignation, tiredness, untidiness, irresponsibility and finally a childish softening with a tendency to alcohol and even more dangerous things.'[1] But the education of the Anima has a positive influence on all spheres. 'It is a great and infinite experience that is given to us, a know-ledge of the world, the fullness and radiance of all knowledge.'[2] According to Jung, the 'woman of Europe' suffers because man cannot appease her hunger for spiritual 'relationship'. Man is only intent on objective 'interests'.[3] But self-education of the Anima function increases the capacity for satisfying the psychic demands of marriage, by cultivating the emotions and making them amenable to more refined forms.

Like an enclosed capsule the theory of the Anima contains further secrets. Whoever opens it breaks through the psychic layer of the projection to the personal encounter. In Jung's theory it is not opened explicitly and therefore his knowledge of the Anima is open to abuse. When it is abused the ring of loneliness is not penetrated at all, the partner merely supplements the Self and is degraded to a mere means in the individua-tion process. This refined form of self-relationship shows how individuation can only lead to 'oneself' if it remains ensnared in psychology. Jung's theory does not lead

[1] *Über den Archetypus*, p. 274.
[2] Rainer Maria Rilke, *Briefe an einen jungen Dichter*, Inselbücherei, p. 24.
[3] *Die Frau von Europa*, p. 26.

beyond it but it does show how it can be followed up and the purpose of the present work was to point to the positive significance of Jung's theory.

To meet the objection that the I–Thou relationship is only seen from the sexual angle, it may be said that the various steps in the process of individuation can only be separated conceptually for the purposes of exposition, whereas in fact in the dynamics of the spiritual life they all flow into one another and form a whole. Consequently our communal relationships with our fellow men, for example, our social relationships, will enter into the education of the Anima and vice versa. On the other hand, however, the education of the Anima acquires a special importance because it represents the unique and necessary passage to the deeper strata of the collective unconscious, in which the predisposition for communal life reposes. The Anima establishes the connection with this predisposition. Anyone who avoids the Anima and fails in the I–Thou relationship will also break down in the I–We relationship, the third step in the process of individuation. His communal life and social integration will suffer: either he will only want to make his own way in life, to be on top, or he will become submerged in the mass and follow every whim of public opinion. Both will have an unfavourable effect on the formation of conscience. Such people do not live their own lives at all, they are 'lived' for them—without their noticing the fact. Their gift for communion with others is crude, uncultivated and devoid of any spiritual aim. The experiences which result from the education of the Anima, on the other hand, make it possible to mould the predisposition for social life in such a way that the personality confronts the community objectively and can serve it objectively, and all the better because it is more widely in possession of its own energies and abilities. Individuation does not in fact lead to individualism. Individuation guides the basic inner predisposition to its goal, to individuality. Just as in medieval ethics individuality did not represent a self-contained being but found fulfilment only in the affirmation of its own being *and* in its incorporation in the whole of Being; and just as modern phenomenology has recognized that the individual person can only build up his own inner spiritual world if man as a person opens himself to the world of his fellow men, so in just the same way Jung sees the process of individuation in which man becomes a Self leading to the Object, to the Other, to the Community. The more the community is made up of personalities, the higher its level will be. As in all living relationships the relationship between personalities and community is not a simple, but a polar relationship. The building up of the personality can only take place within a polar relationship to the community. Thus the task which individuation sets the education of the Self is at the same time a service to the community. It is both an internal, subjective process of integration and also an objective process of relationship and it leads to the fulfilment of individuality by integration with the community, not, it is true, by mere adaptation of the individual to the community, but in the sense of a social 'order' by making us able and ready to recognize and occupy the position which it behoves us to occupy and also to endure the fruitful tension between the ego and the community. The experience of community leads us to the final stage in the process of individuation. Involvement in the interweaving relationships of human societies raises the question as to their meaning. To understand the suprapersonal meaning of the Whole is not an affair of the mind but can come only through life itself. The cosmic-religious problem stands waiting at the end of the way. And anyone who has fought his way so far, in him there can be born a new organ which will enable him to turn consciously to the religious sphere. Thus individuation leads directly to the sphere of religious activity.

CHAPTER FIVE

THE CURE OF SOULS

IN the chapter on Jung's anthropology it was emphasized that his psychology comes very close to a personalist view of man, since the Self denotes the secret creative centre of the soul, which is called the nucleus of the personality in philosophy; but it must also be realized that, given Jung's philosophical presuppositions, the person is not completely actualized although individuation does make it possible to build up the personality. The absolutized Self revolves around itself in self-satisfied isolation. But if the personality is to open its eyes it must confront a Thou. If the psychological theory of individuation is detached from the limitations imposed by Jung's presuppositions and translated into Christian terms, it means no less than that the Self is confronted with the divine Person in the Son of God. The human person can only be completely actualized by the decision that is required by this supreme I–Thou relationship to which all human relationships ultimately point. In this relationship the Self becomes a Thou and the personality takes the step forward to particularity.

If the Christian cure of souls prepares the way for this process in individual people, it is clear that Jung's psychology can perform a most valuable service, though only in the forecourts, by helping to fulfil the natural preconditions for Christian decision and Christian life. Having made clear this basic limitation we shall now suggest some ways in which depth psychology can be of use in the cure of souls. To derive rules and directions for the cure of souls from Jung's analytical psychology would imply a grave misunderstanding of his work. If that work is to bear fruit in priestly activity, it can only do so by means of and through the personality of the priest himself. The synthetic building-up of the personality by the process of individuation is first of all a guide to the formation of the natural priestly man. But that does not mean merely trying out the process: individuation demands the devotion of the whole man; it involves the inner life in a hazardous enterprise. A few words from Laros will indicate the place and the meaning of this natural formation of life:

'Since the whole natural man is called on with all his powers and destined to be the material ground of Grace the development of all genuine humanity, its natural gifts and virtues, its predisposition and capacity for truth, goodness and beauty is the precondition for the creative development of the new man in Christ. One cannot be a twisted, half man, lacking in the natural qualities of pure humanity and, as a sort of supernatural compensation, a whole Christian at the same time.'[1]

What the priest himself has experienced and what he himself has become makes him able to know objectively and to correct those who are entrusted to him. He acquires a feeling for true spiritual health, for what ought to be and what is lacking. Compared with that all the methods and theories he has learnt are of secondary importance. Jung himself gives every beginner this advice: 'Learn your theories as well as you can, but leave them on one side when you meet the miracle of the living soul. The all-important thing is your own creative personality, not mere theory.' The man consecrated to the priesthood must act like a natural 'rectifier'. His

[1] Matthias Laros, *Pfingstgeist Über uns*, Regensburg, 1935, p. 195.

activity will not be merely the application of a dry as dust method acquired by learning but a living radiation of his own personality. 'You must be the kind of person you want to be effective as' (Jung). The first thing, therefore, that depth psychology can give the priest is a 'psychological revival' in himself: a first-hand knowledge of spiritual processes, of the relationships between the various powers within the soul and their polarity.

Jung's theory provides a further stimulus in the educational field. The investigation of neuroses has shown that mistakes in the education of childhood and youth can have life-long after-effects. Education in youth should lay the foundations for the later self-education of the adult. The importance of Jung's theory for this work, in which the priest has often to lend a hand, has already been described in the chapter on Education. The priest will be able to apply his knowledge of depth psychology in the pastoral treatment of neurotics. The priest will rarely be able to avoid therapeutical treatment—treatment which in the truest sense makes the patient whole (= holy). It is not so much a question of serious neurotics —he must leave them to the psychotherapist—but rather the everyday strains and aberrations of the 'heart' which he has to deal with. To examine the spiritual situation, to intervene redemptively and to open the patient's eyes to all the natural conditions of the spiritual life, is the most important groundwork towards the formation of a right conscience and a religious outlook in general. Knowledge of Jung's types will lead to a preventive and differentiated application of ascetic methods. For example, an introverted person with a tendency to brooding should not be encouraged to examine his conscience daily, whereas such examination

will be of great importance for the extroverted person
who tends to lose himself in the external world.

Analytical psychology can provide the priest with most
important insights derived from direct concern with the
religious life. It has to be conceded that Jung has insight
into and experience of the 'spiritual problems of the
present age'. When, therefore, he describes individuation
as the way to a religious life, when he speaks of individual
religious culture, and of modern man's demand for first-
hand experience, it is possible to draw certain conclusions of relevance to the work of the priest. For most
modern men and women religious decisions can no longer
be attained by communal experience or tradition;
they must take place in the solitude of self-discovery.
Jung's work shows that religion is closely connected
with individuation. The process of individuation
heightens a man's ability to live a religious life. From the
Christian standpoint it may be said that individuation
serves the realization of faith. The religious problem of
many people is that they would like to believe, but
cannot conceive faith as a reality. They feel that their
attitude to religion is unauthentic, provisional, that it
has not evolved from the core of their personality. No
pastoral effort that is based merely on theological
doctrine can help them overcome their difficulty since
such people lack the capacity to respond to a purely
theological approach: their spiritual life is undeveloped.
In this context Jung is quite right: 'God himself cannot
thrive in a humanity that is psychically under-
nourished.'[1]

The aim of spiritual guidance must therefore be to
help the patient tread the path of individuation, so that

[1] *Die Frau von Europa*, p. 45 (= *Woman in Europe*, p. 188, in *Contributions to Analytical Psychology*, 1928).

he can acquire for himself the 'first-hand experience' of religion. In the formation of a Christian life, however, every step in the process of individuation leads to a new confrontation with the words of the Gospel and a new need to make a decision for the Gospel. In this way spiritual growth and religious decision will both be at the 'centre' and the danger of one overwhelming the other is avoided. It will then be possible too to bring the 'psychic material' into touch with the contents of faith so that faith will be permeated by the newly acquired symbolic power and sustained by the capacity for numinous experience. From the solitary, individual decision a vision of things shared with others will wrestle its way to the light of day and a striving after the Church will begin. In accordance with Jung's statements about the psyche of modern man, we see the future of the ministry as consisting more than hitherto in a growing pastoral concern for the individual, in the guidance of souls and in religious conversation. The priest knows that in this field all he can do is be a helpful companion. 'But the frontier of the human is always the place where God comes flooding in.'[1] The priest is thereby preserved from too black and also too bright a view of reality. The fruit of this insight is that quality for which the great pastors and priests have always been praised: the quality of goodness.

[1] Gertrud von Lefort, *Die ewige Frau*, Munich, 1934, p. 122.

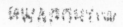